The Encyclopaedia of Tennis

THE ENCYCLOPAEDIA OF TENNIS

YOGRAJ THANI

GYAN
GYAN PUBLISHING HOUSE
NEW DELHI-110 002

GYAN PUBLISHING HOUSE
5 Ansari Road
New Delhi 110 002

ISBN 81-212-0432-1

1993

PRINTED IN INDIA

Published by Mrs. Gayatri Garg for Gyan Publishing House, New Delhi 110002.
Printed at Goyal Offset Works, Delhi.

FOREWORD

Sports develop a language of their own. Tennis is no exception. What is a point penalty, a chop, Service, Ace? Words full of signficance to the tennis world. With this book Lokesh Thani has provided the answer. He has produced an excellent reference work.

This book not only probes the rich history of the game and describes vivid personalities past and present, but also gives practical details of the equipment required, strokes, tactics and rules. It provides a good general background for the enthusiast and for the beginner. There is a detailed Records Section.

Mukesh Kumar

A

A.T.P.

The Association of Tennis Professionals. An organization of male professional tennis players.

A.T.P. computer rankings

A ranking system based on the results of every male touring player.

Ace

A service which the receiver cannot touch. Some consider a service which the receiver touches with his racket, but without any chance of returning it, as an ace, but this should really be classed as a service winner.

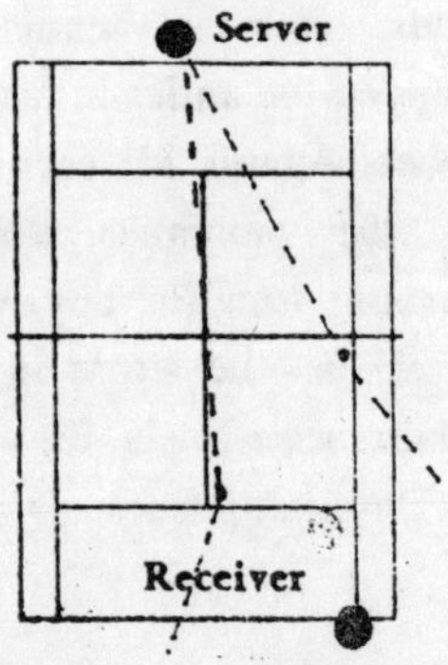

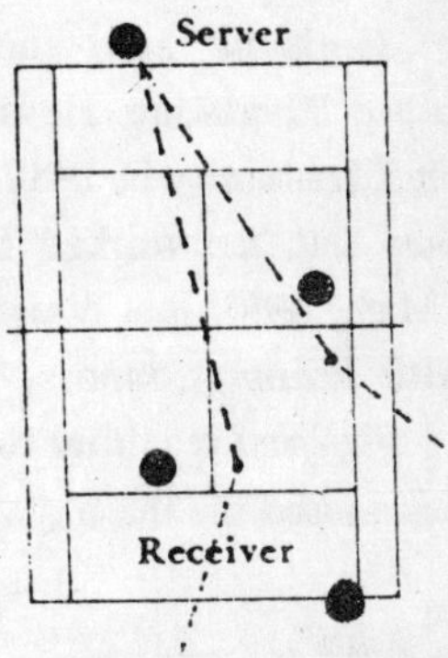

Ace on service

A hard-hit ball impossible to touch with a racket.

Ad

An abbreviated form of the word "Advantage".

Ad in

Is scoring, abbreviation for "advantage server".

Ad out

In scoring, abbreviation for "advantage receiver".

Advantage

After a game has gone to deuce, the player who is a point ahead is said to have 'advantage'. If he wins the next point he wins the game: if he loses, the score reverts to deuce.

Advantage in

One point won by the server after the 40-all mark.

Agassi, Andre

USA (born 1970) — The slightly built young man with the frightening forehand and the most famous man in tennis may command a top 10 ranking. He may have dropped the antics in favour of Born Again Christianity in 1987, but otherwise Agassi has carried the individualism that has worked for him into the pro ranks, which he entered in May, 1986, just two days after turning 16. The boy who, at four, hit with Jimmy Connors, rose to No. 3 in the world in 1988, winning six titles and reaching two Grand Slam semi-finals. He was the No. 1 American and the main man in the US Davis Cup team.

Alexander, John

Australia (born 1951) — A powerful server, he also performs surprisingly well on clay considering his upbringing. He became the youngest player ever to compete in a Davis Cup Challenge round when Harry Hopman pitched him into the match against the US as a 17-year-old in 1968. He reached No. 8 in the world in 1975.

All
In tennis this word means an even score. Within a game 15-15 is 15-all and 30-30 is 30-all. In a set a level game score is called one-all, two-all, three-all.

All-court game
A term usually applied to ability of a player to play all the strokes, from any part of the court. All-around play means a good ground game supplemented by a good net game.

All England Club
The venue for Wimbledon.

Alley
The area on each side of the singles court employed to enlarge the court for doubles play.

Alley or tramlines
Those parts of the court lying between the lines marking the lateral extremities of the singles and doubles courts.

Allison, Wilmer Lawson
USA (1904-1977) — One of the greatest and most spectacular of American doubles specialists, he also gained some notable singles successes. Possessing a fierce smash, a serve 'with the kick of a Taxas mustang', considerable power on the volley, and a fine backhand drive, he found an ideal doubles partner in John Van Ryn. He won at Wimbledon in 1929-30. They took the US title in 1931 and 1935.

Amateur

One who does not receive, or has not received, directly or indirectly, pecuniary advantage by the playing, teaching, demonstrating, or pursuit of the game of tennis.

American Tennis Association

The governing body for Black American players, founded in 1916. It first held singles championships for men and women in 1917.

American twist

An advanced serve in which the racket strikes the ball with an upward and sideward motion causing the ball to spin during its flight and to take a high bounce, usually to the receiver's backhand.

Amritraj, Anand

India (born 1952) — Elder brother of Vijay and Ashok, Anand has failed to fulfil his early promise. He made his Davis Cup debut for India in 1968 and led them to the final in 1974, when they refused to play South Africa because of their apartheid policy. Fine doubles player.

Amritraj, Vijay

India (born 1953) — Vijay, whose name means 'victory' in Hindi, burst onto the scene in 1973 at the age of 20, when he reached the quarter-finals of Wimbledon and US Open. Wimbledon has been the stage for some of his most spectacular matches: in 1979 he led Borg two sets to one and 5-4 in the fourth set tie-break before losing; and in 1981 he was two sets to love up on Jimmy Connors in the quarter-final before Jimbo recovered to win in five. With brothers Anand and Ashok he owns Amritraj Productions, a film company in Hollywood. He has beaten all the top players, from Laver and Rosewall through to Borg and McEnroe. He led Los Angeles Strings to the 1978 World Team Tennis title and had been a member of India's Davis Cup side since 1968 to 1988.

Angle game

A style of play in which the angles of the court are used. Specifically, it refers to the short angles. E.g., the player hits a forehand cross court which lands inside his opponent's service line and close to the opponent's forehand sideline.

Angle volley

A volleying stroke angled past an opponent.

Annie Soisbault Cup

International team competition for women under 21. Match format 2 singles, 1 doubles. First held in 1965.

Anticipatory position

A position assumed while waiting for the ball to be served or returned.

Approach shot

A hard, deep-to-the-corner shot that puts an opponent on the defensive. A type of forcing shot.

Argentina

The Association Argentina de Tennis was founded on 2 September, 1921. The most important event organized by the A.A.T. is the Championship of the Republic, an open championship that forms part of the I.L.T.F. Grand Prix, in which most of the world's best players compete.

Arias, Jimmy

USA (born 1964) — He shares an unusual record with a fellow American, Andrea Jaeger, in that they are the youngest winners of a major open championship. Jimmy was 16 years 296 days and Andrea was 15 years 339 days when they captured the mixed doubles title at the French Open in June 1981. In the 1983 US Open he defeated Yanick Noah to reach the semi-finals, where he was overpowered by Ivan Lendl in straight sets.

Arjuna Awards

The Arjuna Award confers the highest recognition of the Government of India on a sportsperson. Since its institution in 1961, for a sportsperson to be considered for the Arjuna Award, he or she should have given outstanding performances at the national and international levels for three years prior to the year for which the person is being considered for the Award and, in that year, in particular, the person should have achieved excellence in his or her specific discipline of sports. Besides, the sportsperson should have displayed a high sense of discipline, sportsmanship and the best qualities of leadership.

The Arjuna Award carries with it an amount of Rs. 5,000/- a scroll, a blazer, a tie and a bronze statuette of Arjuna.

Arjuna Awards winners

1961 Ramanathan Krishnan
1963 Naresh Kumar
1966 Jaideep Mukherjee
1967 Premjit Lall
1974 Vijay Amritraj
1978-79 Nirupama Mankad
1980-81 Ramesh Krishnan
1985 Anand Amritraj

Asboth, Joseph

Hungary (born 1917) — A stylish right-hander whose victory in the 1947 French singles, when he beat Petra, Tom Brown and Sturgess, was Hungary's most important tennis success before their victory in the Saab King's Cup in 1976. From 1938-57 he played 41 Davis Cup rubbers in 16 ties.

Ashe, Arthur Robert

USA (born 1943) — A cool, thoughtful, dogged competitor, he was the first black American to win the Wimbledon men's singles title and, in 1968, playing as an amateur, he became the first US Open champion.

Always happier on fast courts, he tried hard to succeed on clay but endured regular disappointments in Paris and never progressed further than the semi-finals (1971) in Rome. Between 1963 and 1978, he appeared in 18 Davis Cup ties, winning 27 out of 32 singles and one of two doubles.

Aussem, Fraulein Cilly

Germany (1909-1963) — Later the Contessa della Corta Brae. The only German to win the women's singles at Wimbledon. Her strokes were not strong but she was a model of steadiness and persistence. 'Quite small and more of a girl in appearance with round brown eyes and a cherub face', wrote Helen Wills. 'Her agility on court and the distance that she covers in spite of her shortness are really astonishing.'

Austin, Henry Wilfred

UK (born 1906) — The most successful British man player (after Fred Perry) between the two world wars. Possessed classic ground strokes but lacked overhand power. Was losing singles finalist at Wimbledon to Ellisworth Vines (1932), to J.D. Budge (1938). Was a Wimbledon quarter-finalist (or better) 10 times in the 11 years 1929 to 1939.

Austin, Tracy

USA (born 1962) — In January 1977 she became the youngest player to capture a professional singles title when she won the Avon Futures of Portland. Two years later her precious skills made her the youngest ever US Open champion at the age of 16 years and 9 months. Her total of 25 American junior titles is a record.

Australian Championships

The first Australian championships were held in 1905, and it was not until 1925 that the title changed to its present style.

Men's Singles

1919	A.R.F. Kingscot	UK
1920	P.O'Hara Wood	AUS

1921	R.H. Gemmell	AUS
1922	J.O. Anderson	AUS
1923	P.O'Hara Wood	AUS
1924	J.O. Anderson	AUS
1925	J.O. Anderson	AUS
1926	J.B. Hawkes	AUS
1927	G.L. Patterson	AUS
1928	J. Borotra	FRA
1929	J.C. Gregory	UK
1930	E.F. Moon	AUS
1931	J.H. Crawford	AUS
1932	J.H. Crawford	AUS
1933	J.H. Crawford	AUS
1934	F.J. Perry	UK
1935	J.H. Crawford	AUS
1936	A.K. Quist	AUS
1937	V.B. McGrath	AUS
1938	J.D. Budge	USA
1939	J.E. Bromwich	AUS
1940	A.K. Quist	AUS
1941	Not held	
1942	Not held	
1943	Not held	
1944	Not held	
1945	Not held	
1946	J.E. Bromwich	AUS
1947	D. Pails	AUS
1948	A.K. Quist	AUS
1949	F.A. Sedgman	AUS
1950	F.A. Sedgman	AUS
1951	R. Savitt	USA
1952	K. McGregor	AUS
1953	K.R. Rosewall	AUS
1954	M.G. Rose	AUS

1955	K.R. Rosewall	AUS
1956	L.A. Hoad	AUS
1957	A.J. Cooper	AUS
1958	A.J. Cooper	AUS
1959	A. Olmedo	USA
1960	R.G. Laver	AUS
1961	R.S. Emerson	AUS
1962	R.G. Laver	AUS
1963	R.S. Emerson	AUS
1964	R.S. Emerson	AUS
1965	R.S. Emerson	AUS
1966	R.S. Emerson	AUS
1967	R.S. Emerson	AUS
1968	W.W. Bowrey	AUS
1969	R.G. Laver	AUS
1970	A.R. Ashe	USA
1971	K.R. Rosewall	AUS
1972	K.R. Rosewall	AUS
1973	J.D. Newcombe	AUS
1974	J.S. Connors	USA
1975	J.D. Newcombe	AUS
1976	M.R. Edmondson	AUS
1977	R. Tanner	USA
1978	G. Vilas	ARG
1979	G. Vilas	ARG
1980	B. Teacher	USA
1981	J.C. Kriek	SA
1982	J.C. Kriek	SA
1983	M. Wilander	SWE
1984	M. Wilander	SWE
1985	S. Edberg	SWE
1986	Not held	
1987	S. Edberg	SWE
1988	M. Wilander	SWE

1989	Ivan Lendl	CZ
1990	Ivan Lendl	CZ

Women's Singles

1922	M. Molesworth	AUS
1923	M. Molesworth	AUS
1924	S. Lance	AUS
1925	D. Akhurst	AUS
1926	D. Akhurst	AUS
1927	E.F. Boyd	AUS
1928	D. Akhurst	AUS
1929	D. Akhurst	AUS
1930	D. Akhurst	AUS
1931	C. Buttsworth	AUS
1932	C. Buttsworth	AUS
1933	J. Hartigan	AUS
1934	J. Hartigan	AUS
1935	D.E. Round	UK
1936	J. Hartigan	AUS
1937	N. Wynne	AUS
1938	D.M. Bundy	USA
1939	E. Westacott	AUS
1940	N. Bolton	AUS
1941	Not held	
1942	Not held	
1943	Not held	
1944	Not held	
1945	Not held	
1946	N. Bolton	AUS
1947	N. Bolton	AUS
1948	N. Bolton	AUS
1949	D.J. Hatt	USA
1950	A.L. Brough	USA
1951	N. Bolton	AUS

		Australian
1952	T. Long	AUS
1953	M.C. Connolly	USA
1954	T. Long	AUS
1955	B. Penrose	AUS
1956	M. Carter	AUS
1957	S.J. Fry	USA
1958	A. Mortimer	UK
1959	M. Reitano	AUS
1960	M. Smith	AUS
1961	M. Smith	AUS
1962	M. Smith	AUS
1963	M. Smith	AUS
1964	M. Smith	AUS
1965	M. Smith	AUS
1966	M. Smith	AUS
1967	N. Richey	USA
1968	B.J. King	USA
1969	M. Court	AUS
1970	M. Court	AUS
1971	M. Court	AUS
1972	S.V. Wade	UK
1973	M. Court	AUS
1974	E.F. Goolagong	AUS
1975	E.F. Goolagong	AUS
1976	E.F. Cawley	AUS
1977	K. Reid	AUS
1978	C.O'Neil	AUS
1979	B.K. Jordan	USA
1980	Hana Mandlikova	CZ
1981	M. Navratilova	USA
1982	C. Lloyd	USA
1983	M. Navratilova	USA
1984	C. Lloyd	USA
1985	M. Navratilova	USA

1986	Not held	
1987	Hana Mandlikova	CZ
1988	Steffi Graf	W. GER
1989	Steffi Graf	W. GER
1990	Steffi Graf	W. GER

Men's Doubles

1946	John Bromwich, Adrian Quist	AUS
1947	John Bromwich, Adrian Quist	AUS
1948	John Bromwich, Adrian Quist	AUS
1949	John Bromwich, Adrian Quist	AUS
1950	John Bromwich, Adrian Quist	AUS
1951	Ken McGregor, Frank Sedgman	AUS
1952	Ken McGregor, Frank Sedgman	AUS
1953	Lew Hoad, Ken Rose	AUS
1954	Rex Hartwig, Mervyn Rose	AUS
1955	Vic Seixas, Tony Trabert	USA
1956	Lew Hoad, Ken Rosewall	AUS
1957	Neale Fraser, Lew Hoad	AUS
1958	Ashley Cooper, Neale Fraser	AUS
1959	Rod Laver, Robert Mark	AUS
1960	Rod Laver, Robert Mark	AUS
1961	Rod Laver, Robert Mark	AUS
1962	Roy Emerson, Neale Fraser	AUS
1963	Bob Hewitt, Fred Stolle	AUS
1964	Bob Hewitt, Fred Stolle	AUS
1965	John Newcombe, Tony Roche	AUS
1966	Roy Emerson, Fred Stolle	AUS
1967	John Newcombe, Tony Roche	AUS
1968	Dick Crealy, Allan Stone	AUS
1969	Roy Emerson, Rod Laver	AUS
1970	Bob Lutz, Stan Smith	USA
1971	John Newcombe, Tony Roche	AUS
1972	Owen Davidson, Ken Rosewall	AUS

1973	Mal Anderson, John Newcombe	AUS
1974	Ross Case, Geoff Masters	AUS
1975	John Alexamder, Phil Dent	AUS
1976	John Newcombe, Tony Roche	AUS
1977	Arthur Ashe (USA), Tony Roche	AUS
	Ray Ruffels, Allan Stone	AUS
1978	Wotek Fibak (Pol), Kim Warwick	AUS
1979	Peter McNamara, Paul McNamee	AUS
1980	Mark Edmondson, Kim Warwick	AUS
1981	Mark Edmondson, Kim Warwick	AUS
1982	John Alexander, John Fitzgerald	AUS
1983	Mark Edmondson, Paul McNamee	AUS
1984	Mark Edmondson (AUS), Sherwood Stewart	USA
1985	Paul Annacone (USA), Christo Van Rensburg	S.AF
1986	Not held	
1987	Stefan Edberg, Anders Jarryd	SWE
1988	Rick Leach, Jim Pugh	USA
1989	Rick Leach, Jim Pugh	USA
1990	Pieter Aldrich, Dannie Visser	S.AF

Women's Doubles

1946	Mary Bevis, Joyce Fitch	AUS
1947	Nancye Bolton, Thelma Long	AUS
1948	Nancye Bolton, Thelma Long	AUS
1949	Nancye Bolton, Thelma Long	AUS
1950	Louise Brough, Doris Hart	USA
1951	Nancye Bolton, Thelma Long	AUS
1952	Nancye Bolton, Thelma Long	AUS
1953	Maureen Connolly, Julie Sampson	USA
1954	Mary Howton (nee Bevis), Beryl Penrose	AUS
1955	Mary Hawton, Beryl Penrose	AUS
1956	Mary Hawton, Thelma Long	AUS
1957	Shirley Fry, Althea Gibson	USA
1958	Mary Hawton, Thelma Long	AUS

1959	Sandra Reynolds, Renee Schuurman	SAF
1960	Maria Bueno (Bra), Christine Truman	UK
1961	Mary Reitano, Margaret Smith	AUS
1962	Robyn Ebbern, Margaret Smith	AUS
1963	Robyn Ebbern, Margaret Smith	AUS
1964	Judy Tegart, Lesley Turner	AUS
1965	Margaret Smith, Lesley Turner	AUS
1966	Carole Graebner, Nancy Richey	USA
1967	Judy Tegart, Lesley Turner	AUS
1968	Karen Krantzcke, Kerry Melville	AUS
1969	Margaret Court (nee Smith), Judy Tegart	AUS
1970	Margaret Court, Judy Dalton (nee Tegart)	AUS
1971	Margaret Court, Evonne Goolagong	AUS
1972	Helen Gourlay, Kerry Harris	AUS
1973	Margaret Court (Aus) Virginia Wade	UK
1974	Evonne Goolagong (Aus), Peggy Michel	USA
1975	Evonne Goolagong (Aus), Peggy Michel	USA
1976	Evonne Cawley (nee Goolagong), Helen Gourlay	AUS
1977	Diane Fromholtz, Helen Gourlay	AUS
	Evonne Cawley, Helen Cawley (Aus) shared the December title with Ramona Guerrant (USA), Kerry Reid (nee Melville) (Aus) Final not played.	
1978	Betsy Nagelsen (USA), Renata Tomanova	CS
1979	Judith Chaloner (NZ), Dianne Evers	AUS
1980	Betsy Nagelsen (USA), Martina Navratilova	CS
1981	Kathy Jordan, Anne Smith	USA
1982	Martina Navratilova, Pam Shriver	USA
1983	Martina Navratilova, Pam Shriver	USA
1984	Martina Navratilova, Pam Shriver	USA
1985	Martina Navratilova, Pam Shriver	USA
1986	Not held	
1987	Martina Navratilova, Pam Shriver	USA
1988	Martina Navratilova, Pam Shriver	USA
1989	Martina Navratilova, Pam Shriver	USA

	Australian

1990	Helena Sukova, Jana Novotna	CZ

Mixed Doubles

1946	Colin Long, Nancye Bolton	AUS
1947	Colin Long, Nancye Bolton	AUS
1948	Colin Long, Nancye Bolton	AUS
1949	Frank Sedgman (Aus), Doris Hart	USA
1950	Frank Sedgman (Aus), Doris Hart	USA
1951	George Worthington , Thelma Long	AUS
1952	George Worthington, Thelma Long	AUS
1953	Rex Hartwig (Aus), Julie Sampson	USA
1954	Rex Hartwig, Thelma Long	AUS
1955	George Worthington, Thelma Long	AUS
1956	Neale Fraser, Beryl Penrose	AUS
1957	Mal Anderson, Fay Muller	AUS
1958	Bob Howe, Mary Howton	AUS
1959	Robert Mark (Aus), Sandra Reynolds	S. AF
1960	Trevor Fancutt (S. Af), Jan Lehane	AUS
1961	Bob Hewitt, Jan Lehane	AUS
1962	Fred Stolle, Lesley Turner	AUS
1963	Ken Fletcher, Margaret Smith	AUS
1964	Ken Fletcher, Margaret Smith	AUS
1965	John Newcombe, Margaret Smith (Aus) shared title with Owen Davidson, Robyn Ebbern (Aus). Final not played.	
1966	Tony Roche, Judy Tegart	AUS
1967	Owen Davidson , Lesley Turner	AUS
1968	Dick Crealy (Aus), Billie Jean King	USA
1969	Marty Riessen (USA), Margaret Court (nee Smith) (Aus) shared title with Fred Stolle (Aus), Ann Jones (UK) . Final not played.	
1970	Not held	
1971	Not held	
1972	Not held	
1973	Not held	

1974	Not held	
1975	Not held	
1976	Not held	
1977	Not held	
1978	Not held	
1979	Not held	
1980	Not held	
1981	Not held	
1982	Not held	
1983	Not held	
1984	Not held	
1985	Not held	
1986	Not held	
1987	Sherwood Stewart, Zina Garrison	USA
1988	Jim Pugh (USA), Jana Novotna	CZ
1989	Jim Pugh (USA), Jana Novotna	CZ

Australian formation

A positioning of players in a doubles game in which the server's partner stands on the same side of court from which he is serving.

Ayala, Luis

Chile (born 1932) — Chile's most prominent man player. Became a contracted professional in 1961.

B

B.P. Cup

International team championship on indoor courts for players under 21. Format: 2 singles, 1 doubles, except for final when reverse singles were played. First held in 1973.

Backcourt

The area between the base line and service line.

Backhand

A stroke made with the playing arm and racket across the body. Any stroke played on the left side of a right-handed player, or on the right side of a left-handed player.

Backhand drive

Readiness position as in the forehand drive. The body starts to twist, left shoulder backwards. The racket is lightly rested on the left hand. As the player runs towards the ball, he begins his swing. He takes the

racket back with his left hand so that it points diagonally up and backwards and lies close to the body- start of the curve. At this stage, the right wrist moves slightly to the
left.

Backhand grip

While there is some disagreement by the experts on the best method of grasping the racket for the forehand stroke, there is little or none on the backhand. Almost all use the modified Eastern backhand for this stroke.

Backhand grip

The Eastern backhand grip is obtained by placing the palm on the top plane so that a check mark is formed between the forefinger and thumb. In this position the first knuckle of the index finger is on the top plane of the handle.

The backhand grip can be obtained from the Eastern forehand grip by shifting the hand to the left (counterclockwise) about one quarter of a turn. This should bring the back knuckle of the first finger directly on top of the racket.

Backhand shot
Stroke played with the reverse side of the racket, i.e. with the back of the hand facing the ball.

Backhand stroke, double-handed
A backhand stroke in which the player keeps both hands on the handle throughout the stroke. This aids power and control, but reduces reach.

Back room
The space between the base line and the court's backstop or fence. Also called run-back.

Backspin

Spin applied to the ball by hitting down behind it, causing the ball to spin in the opposite direction from its flight.

Backstop

The netting or canvas at the back of the court. Under championship conditions this must be at least 21 feet from the baseline.

Backswing

The beginning of all ground strokes and service motion requiring a backswing to greater energy for the forward swing.

Bad ball

A ball that does not land in the playing court area.

Baddeley, Wilfred

UK (born 1872) — Youngest winner of the Wimbledon men's singles in 1891 aged 19 years 5 months 23 days.

Ball

The cloth-covered sphere used in playing tennis. Also the term used for the result of a stroke. Thus, a "good-length ball" is a stroke which makes the ball hit the ground near the base line.

Ballboy or ballgirl

Boy or girl with the duty of collecting stray balls around the court and feeding them to the players.

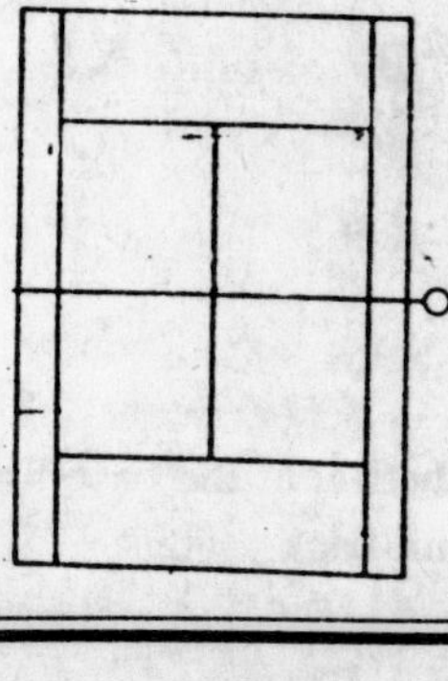

Band

The strip of canvas attached to the top of the net.

Barker, Sue

UK (born 1956) — Barker's main weapon was a forehand drive of formidable strength. Blonde and vivacious, she had excellent mobility, but her game was erratic, and when she was off form she suffered ignominious defeats, including a number of first round losses at Wimbledon, where British players are always under pressure. Barker won the Swedish and Swiss titles in 1975, then came her best year, 1976, when she won the French and German Opens and was runner-up in the British Hard Court Championships. In 1977 she proved she could measure up with the best, winning back-to-back titles on the Virginia Slims tour at San Francisco and Dallas, and beating Martina Navratilova before losing a three-set title match against Chris Evert in the Slims finals.

Barrett, H. Roper

UK (born 1873) — Wimbledon doubles champion in 1909, 1912 and 1913 with A.W. Gore.

Baseliner

A player who operates from the back of the court.

Base-line game

A style of play in which the player stays at or near the base line and seldom moves to the forecourt or net.

Becker, Boris

W. Germany (born 1967) — Wimbledon 1985 was where the world witnessed the birth of Boris Becker, tennis superstar. When he defeated Kevin Curren on that warm Sunday afternoon, the heavily-built 17-year-old set not one record but three. As well as being the youngest champion, he was also the first German and the first non-seed to triumph. It is pretty difficult to fluke seven wins over a Wimbledon fortnight, but just to displace any doubt, Becker repeated the feat in 1986, still younger than any previous champion.

Becker's highly-publicized split with Gunther Bosch, his

childhood coach and mentor, at the 1987 Australian Open, had him in the tennis doldrums for a year. Eight months elapsed before he next won a tournament — at Indian Wells, California, where he has a house. He won Wimbledon singles in 1985, 1986 and 1989; also won US Open singles in 1989.

Being beaten by the ball

Arriving too late; being passed or almost passed; or too late for optimal position.

Bergelin, Lennart

Sweden (born 1925) — One of the great Swedish players, notable for his exceptional fluency and ease of stroke and accomplishment of high athletic attainment despite being a diabetic. Wimbledon singles quarter-finalist in 1946, 1948 and 1951.

Bernard, Marcel

France (born 1914) — Shrewd and stylish, a canny left-hander with considerable touch, he is one of only two French players to have won in Paris since the days of the Four 'Musketeers' (the other is Noah, 1983); demonstrated his promise early, reaching the French singles final and, with Boussus. Between 1935-56 he played 42 Davis Cup rubbers in 25 ties and he has also served as president of the French Tennis Federation.

Betz, Pauline May

USA (born 1919) — Now Mrs. Addie. An agile, athletic competitor, who might have gained many more titles if the war had not interrupted international competition. She was ranked eighth in the US in 1939 and was the most successful player in wartime competitions there, winning the national title from 1942-44. She won Wimbledon at a cost of only 20 games in 1946.

Big game

A style of play in which the emphasis is on a big service and a net attack.

Big server
A player with a powerful service.

Bingley, Blanche
UK (1863 - 1946) — Winning the Wimbledon women's singles in 1886, 1889, 1894, 1897, 1899 and 1900. Became the wife of G.W. Hillyard, secretary of the All England Lawn Tennis and Croquet Club.

Bird bath
A minor depression in which water settles on a non porous court surface after a rain. Dirt or dust often remains in the depression after the water evaporates. This may cause a ball to skid upon hitting the dust in the bird bath and usually causes deterioration of the court surfacing.

Blocked ball
A ball returned without the swing of a racket, by simply meeting it with a stiff wrist and stationary racket; generally, a "stop-volley.

Borg, Bjorn
Sweden (born 1956) — He is the most popular and intriguing tennis star on the international scene. His icy calm on the courts, together with his shy and sensitive personality, has combined to create something of a legend. Looking back on the milestones in his career, he first started to play tennis at the age of nine. Then in March 1972, aged fifteen, he left school in order to play tennis full-time. The Swedish Tennis Association sent him to their training camp on the Riviera where he was coached by Percy Rosenberg, so that by 1974 Borg's game had established him as one of the world's top tennis players. In 1978 he won the Pepsi Grand Slam, three W.C.T. tournaments, the Suntory Cup in Tokyo, the Italian and French Opens, the Bastad Swedish Open and Wimbledon for the fifth year in succession.

Borotra, Jean

France (born 1898) — Celebrated member of the French 'Four Musketeers' who won the Davis Cup for France 1927 to 1932. A spectacular volleyer and a dominating court personality especially at Wimbledon. In 1946 became a notable administrator at both national and international levels. The 'Bounding Basque' retained his prodigious athletic prowess and was still an active competitive player well into his sixties. His first Davis Cup appearance was in 1922, his last twenty-six years later in 1947.

Borowiak, Jeff

USA (born 1949) — A keen jogger, the long-legged Californian is also an accomplished musician, gaining a major at U.C.L.A. for the flute, piano and clarionet. He was US National Junior Champion in 1967 and runner-up in the prestigious, international junior event, the Orange Bowl in 1968. His best ranking was 25 in 1977. One of the characters of the circuit, Borowiak endeared himself to Wimbledon crowds in 1981, by arriving for the tournament on a battered old bike which he parked by the dressing room wall while he played. The style obviously suited him for he reached the last 16, with victories over Brian Gottfried and Tim Gullikson, before falling to Peter McNamara.

Bound

The bounce of a struck ball from the court surface; the curved path of the ball from first and second impact with the court surface.

B.P. Cup

An international team competition, sponsored by B.P., for men and women under 21 similar to the Galea Cup but for teams of maximum three and held indoors in Britain.

Brasher, Mrs. C.

UK (born 1934) — She won French women's singles in 1957. An unspectacular but resolute competitor, her performance on hard courts brought her world No.3 rating in 1957.

Break
Relates to the act of winning a game in which the opponent serves.

Break point
The receiver's chance to break service. Break points are love-40, 15-40, 30-40 and advantage receiver.

Broken service
A game won by the server's opponent.

Bromwich, John Edward
Australia (born 1918) — A gracefully unorthodox player whose career might have been ever more successful if it had not been interrupted by World War II. Ambidextrous but using both hands on the forehand, he used a very light, softly strung racket to control the ball with great subtlety. He won the Australian singles in 1939 and regained the title from Quist in 1946. Those were his only major singles victories, although he was agonizingly close to success in 1948 Wimbledon when he lost to Falkenburg after leading 5-2 in the finals.

Brookes, Sir Norman Everard
Australia (1877-1968) — One of the all-time greats of the game. A notable volleyer he first came to Wimbledon in 1905 when he lost to Laurie Doherty in the challenge round. In 1907 he became the first overseas player and the first Australian to win Wimbledon men's singles. He and New Zealander Tony Wilding won the Davis Cup for Australia in the same year and their joint skill dominated the men's game until 1914. He reached the last 16 of the singles at Wimbledon in 1924 in his 47th year.

Brough, Althea Louise
USA (born 1923) — Now Mrs. Clapp. An aggressive server and volleyer, she played a major part in establishing American domination of women's tennis immediately after World War II. Won Wimble-

don singles 1948/49/50 and again in 1955 after the retirement of Maureen Connolly, who beat her in 1952 and 1954.

Brown, Geoff

Australia (born 1924) — Famed for his lightning service, a meteoric shot despite his small stature, and a powerful double-fisted forehand drive. Reached all three finals at Wimbledon in 1946 but failed to take a title. He was also a losing finalist in both doubles in 1950 and never did take a major title.

Brugnon, Jacques

France (1895-1978) — The doubles specialist of the 'Four Musketeers', he gained most of his early success with Cochet and then formed a partnership with Borotra, which was still capable of reaching the 1939 French final, when he was 44 and Borotra 40, and coming three times within a point of the title. Played 31 Davis Cup doubles and 6 singles from 1921-34.

Budge, Don

USA (born 1915) — Tall and lean, with a clutch of red hair and freckles, Don Budge could have passed for Huck Finn. His record added to the all-American image. He won both the US and Wimbledon Championships twice, in 1937 and 1938, and compiled an awesome 25-4 won-lost record in Davis Cup play. In 1938, his best year, Budge won the Aussie and French titles in addition to the US and Wimbledon crowns— the sport's first Grand Slam. Three "slam tournaments" are played on grass, an advantage for power players and one that Budge exploited to the fullest. Won US singles and doubles twice each. Won all three events at Wimbledon in 1937 and again in 1938.

Bueno, Maria Esther Andion

Brazil (born 1939) — The most gracefully artistic of post-war women's champions. For nearly a decade her rivalry with Margaret Court provided the principal excitement of the women's game, but at the end she was plagued by injury. Won Wimbledon singles 1959/60/64, and doubles (with Althea Gibson) 1958, (with Darlene Hard) 1960/63, (with Billie Jean King) 1965, and (with Nancy Gunter) 1966, and (with Margaret Court) 1968.

Bullet

A hard-hit ball.

Bundy, May Sutton

UK (1886-1975) — She became the first overseas winner of the Wimbledon singles in 1905. Her daughter Dorothy won the Australian singles in 1938 and in 1979.

Bye

The status of a player who enters the next or subsequent round without playing or without receiving a walk-over from a player drawn to meet him.

C

Cash, Pat

Australia (born 1965) — He won the Wimbledon and US Open junior titles in 1982 and was runner-up in French junior event. He seems to have the techniques, physique and temperament to end Australia's search for another champion. He won the Wimbledon singles in 1987. His best showing in Grand Slam events in 1988 was at the Australian Open, where he lost a close five-set final to Mats Wilander. At Wimbledon he was beaten in straight sets in the quarter-finals by Boris Becker.

Cannonball

An extremely fast, normally spinless service, reaching around 176 km/h.

Cano, Ricardo

Argentina (born 1951) — Cano won recognition throughout South America in 1977 when he inspired Argentina's upset of the United States in the Davis Cup by beating Dick Stockton. But it was not until he had turned 30 in 1981 that the staunch family man made his real breakthrough in world tennis. The clay court specialist had previously preferred to play the South American circuit so as to be close to his wife Claudia and their two daughters, Dolores and Vitoria. His move to the main tour paid immediate dividends as he reached the semi-final in Cairo and six other quarter-finals.

Carry

An illegal shot produced when the ball slides across the racket strings and is in effect thrown over the net.

Cawley, Evonne

Australia (born 1951) — She won Wimbledon women's singles in 1971 and 1980. Won Australian singles in 1974, 1975, 1976 and 1977.

Centre court

The main court in any tennis arena, although Wimbledon's Centre Court is the most celebrated in the game.

Centre line

The line dividing the service court into two halves.

Centre mark

The mark bisecting the base line, defining one of the limits of the service position.

Centre mark

Short mark that bisects the base line.

Centre strap

A strap placed at the centre of the net and anchored to the court to facilitate a constant three feet height for the bet at the centre.

Centre strop

Two-inch-wide piece of canvas that secures the net at the centre of the court on some surfaces.

Centre service line

Divides the service area of the court into halves, the right (forehand; first) and left (backhand; second) service courts.

Chalk

The white material often used to mark lines on some tennis surfaces. When a ball strikes exactly on a line, white dust often flies into the air, and players then speak of seeing chalk, meaning that a disputed ball was good because it raised white dust.

Challenge cups

Trophies offered in lawn tennis, the holders of which are open to challenge for their possession. The customary requirements are that the holder must meet the winner of an event held once each year, and if the trophy be won three times by the same player, it passes into his permanent possession. In England, some of these cups must be won three times in succession, but this is not the case in America.

Challenge round

The final of an event in which the previous winner stands out and awaits the winner of the preliminary series of matches to challenge him for his title.

Challenger

The player who survives a preliminary series of matches and so has the right to 'challenge' the holder of the title at stake.

Chambers, Dorothea Lambert

UK (1883-1960) — The dominant British woman player for more than a decade before World War I and seven times singles champion at Wimbledon. Her loss in the Wimbledon Challenge Round of 1919 to Suzanne Lenglen after having two match balls was one of the most famous matches in the history of lawn tennis. She played for Great Britain in the Wightman Cup in 1926, 23 years after her first Wimbledon singles title in 1903. She became a professional coach in 1928.

Champion barred

The conditions of most events for championships, the holder of the title being debarred from entering for the prizes, and meeting the winner in the challenge round.

Championship

The title held by virtue of winning any tournament held for supremacy of any given section. Also, the event held for the right to challenge for the title or trophy.

Chang, Michael

USA (born 1972) — The pint-sized 17-year-old may seem an unlikely candidate for the top spot, but he already commands a top 10 ranking, a Grand Slam title and no one who saw him surpass Boris Becker as the youngest ever Grand Slam champion at the 1989 French Open would say he lacks the desire or heart for the job. He won French championships in 1989.

Change of length

Tactical ploy in which a player seeks to win points or create openings by varying the length of his shots, such as one short, another long and so on.

Change-of-pace

The game strategy or tactic of changing the speed of your shots or reversing the spin on the ball.

Changing courts

The process whereby players, at the end of every odd game during a set, change to opposite sides of the net.

Chip

A short, usually angled and frequently sliced shot designed mostly to outmanoeuvre the net attacks of a volley.

Choke

Shorten the grip on the racket or to play badly under pressure.

Chop

A stroke made by imparting backspin to the ball. It has similarities with a slice in which the ball is struck diagonally so that a mixture of back and side spin is imparted.

Circuit

Term used when referring to the various tournaments on a player's schedule. Same as tour.

Closed - faced racket

Slanting the racket so that the striking side of the face is tilted towards the ground or, in the case of a service, tilted towards the server during the backswing.

Clothing

Tennis clothes do not have to be expensive. They should be simple, neat, and not restrict your movement. Shorts, loose shirts, white cotton socks, and sneakers are fine. There are also many kinds of tennis outfits for girls.

Official tournament play requires that players wear white clothing. The sneakers should also be white and light rather than heavy. Thick, white cotton socks are also best.

Clubs

The oldest lawn tennis club in the world was the Leamington Lawn Tennis Club in the grounds of the Manor House Hotel, Leamington, Warwickshire, England. It was founded by Major T. H. Gem, Mr. J. B. Perera, Dr. A. Wellesley Tomkins and Dr. F. Haynes in 1872. It is now defunct.

The biggest club in Great Britain is the Hurlingham Club, Fulham, London. It has 20 grass and 20 hard courts, a total of 40.

Cochet, Henri

France (born 1901) — The great instinctive genius of lawn tennis, swift and imaginative, a master of the volley and half-volley, whose play could rise to dizzy heights and sometimes slip to unexpected disaster. Won Wimbledon singles 1927/29 and doubles (with J. Brugnon) 1927/30/32.

Commonwealth Caribbean L.T.A.

Originally called the British Caribbean L.T.A., this association was formed by the L.T.A. of the Bahamas, Barbados, Guyana, Jamaica. Changing its name to the Commonwealth Caribbean L.T.A. in 1970, it provides a team for the Davis Cup and sponsors an annual Inter-Caribbean tournament, the Brandon Trophy.

Concrete courts

Concrete courts are of different designs in different parts of the country, due to variations in climate, slite, subsoil conditions and available cement sand and gravel. In most instances, carefully designed and installed subsoil drainage is required.

Conditioning

That just is not so. Tennis is a physically demanding game, and tennis players have to be in excellent physical condition. Players must dash all over the court to return shots.

Connolly, Maureen

USA (born 1934) — One of the all-time greats of the women's game. She became US singles champion in 1951 at the age of 16. In her subsequent career she was beaten only four times, by Doris Hart at South Orange, New Jersey, in 1952, by Miss Hart again in the Italian championships in 1953, by Shirley Fry in Los Angeles in 1953 and by

Beverly Baker Fleitz at La Jolla, California early in 1954. After winning the US clay courts title in the summer of 1954 she broke her leg while riding and retired from competition, subsequently becoming a coaching professional. Best world ranking No 1 in 1952-54.

Connors, Jimmy

USA (born 1952) — Jimmy Connors reached another milestone in September 1983 when he won the US Open for the fifth time to record the 100th tournament victory of his illustrious career. He has won some magnificent matches and also provided the opposition when several players have enjoyed their finest moments — notably Arthur Ashe in the 1975 Wimbledon final, Manuel Orantes in the 1975 US Open and Guillermo Vilas in the US Open of 1977. His duels with Bjorn Borg will be remembered for their superior quality and impeccable sportsmanship.

Consolation

A prize event, or match, open (in America) to any player beaten in the first match actually played, or (in England) generally to all players beaten in the first and second rounds. Similar to plate, as used abroad.

Continental grip

A racket grip which enables all strokes to be made without changing hand position. It is midway between the orthodox forehand and backhand grips but it demands a strong wrist if it is going to be effective.

Conventional stroking

In the orthodox manner.

Cooper, Ashley

Australia (born 1936) - A classic example of a fine player who succeeded to the game's highest prizes when better colleagues before him because ineligible was Ashley Cooper, a young Australian who, in due course, himself turned professional. There were many good Australians around at that time. Two of the best, Ken Rosewall and Lew Hoad, dominated the scene in the mid-1950s. Hoad won three out of the four Grand Slam titles in 1956, and stayed amateur for another year, although Rosewall deserted the amateur ranks at the end of the season. His great year was 1958. He won the Australian, Wimbledon and US singles — put the Australian, French and US doubles — to make his own case for a worthwhile financial guarantee. He signed on the dotted line at the end of 1958.

County championship

The British Inter-County Championship was instituted for men's teams in 1895 and played as a knock-out competition on grass courts. A similar competition for women was begun in 1899. The format comprises six players a side with three doubles pairs playing each other. In 1925 both events were changed to a league system, divided in groups of six counties with each team playing all others in the same group in the course of one week. Two teams earn promotion or suffer relegation. The Inter-County Championship on Hard Court began for both men and women's teams in 1920 and has been a knock-out event throughout. Six players comprise each team. The men play only singles, twelve in all. Women play six singles and three doubles.

Court

The surface may be grass, variety of asphalt, wood, porous concrete, or other composition. It is marked out with white lines. The lines are included within the limits of the court.

Diagram of the Tennis Court

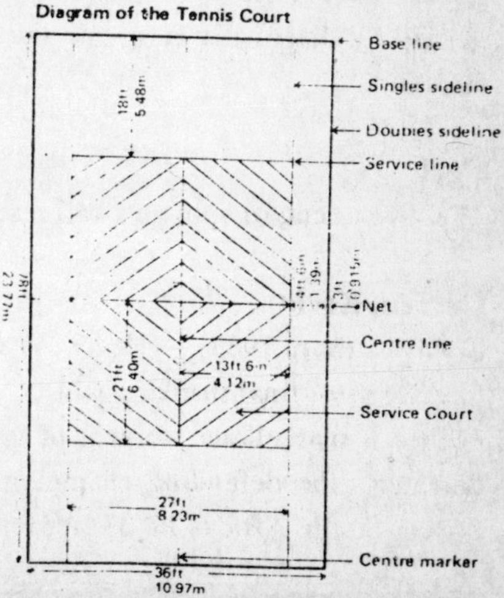

Court material

The surface of the court-grass, clay, hard synthetic, etc.

Cover

Turning the face of the racket from the perpendicular forward, usually giving topspin to the ball.

Covered court

An indoor court for winter play, generally with wood or synthetic surface, always with roof—used chiefly in England. In the United States, called an indoor court.

Crack

A slang expression abbreviated from "Crack-a-Jack," meaning a very expert player.

Cramm, Gottfried von, Baron

Germany (1909-1976) — An elegant stylist and Germany's most successful player. Won French singles 1934/36 and doubles (with H. Henkel) 1937, and German singles 1932/33/34/35/48/49 and doubles 1948/49/53/55. Won 82 Davis Cup rubbers out of 102 in 37 ties between 1932-53.

Cross-court shot

A ball hit diagonally from one side line to the other side line or across the court.

Curl

The twist, cut, or spin on a ball resulting from a sharp cut stroke.

Curren, Kevin

S. Africa (born 1958) — He lost Wimbledon's finest match in 1983 — a five-set semi-final thriller against New Zealand's Chris Lewis — but he had a marvellous moment of glory in the fourth round when he defeated the defending champion, Jimmy Connors. The rangy, raw boned South African hit 33 aces past the finest returner of service in the world to achieve one of the great upsets of the tournament. He lost Wimbledon's final match in 1985 against Boris Becker.

Cut

The twist, spin or curl applied to a ball.

Cut stroke

A stroke in which the racket strikes a glancing blow and is drawn sharply to one side or another in striking.

Cut off the angle

To move forward quickly against an opponent's cross-court shot, allowing the player to hit the ball near the centre of the court rather than near the sidelines.

D

Davidson, Owen Keir

Australia (born 1943) — Coach at the All England Club, Wimbledon. A left-hander and successful mixed doubles player. In 1967 he won the mixed championships of Australia (with Lesley Turner-Bowrey) and (with Billie Jean King) of South Africa, France, Wimbledon and America.

Davis Cup

The idea of presenting this celebrated silver bowl to be won annually by the male representatives of lawn tennis playing countries was conceived by American Dwight Davis (q.v.). As a Harvard student, he played exhibition lawn tennis matches in California and British Columbia in 1899. So successful was this tour with three other college boys, that Davis persuaded his wealthy father to present a trophy which was to be the means of promoting healthy rivalry between Great Britain and America. In the first match in 1900, Davis won a single and a double. This was a two-nation contest.

Year	*Winner*	*Runner-up*	*Venue*
1919	Australasia	British Isles	Sydney
1920	United States	Australasia	Auckland
1921	United States	Japan	New York
1922	United States	Australasia	New York
1923	United States	Australia	New York
1924	United States	Australia	Philadelphia
1925	United States	France	Philadelphia
1926	United States	France	Philadelphia
1927	France	United States	Philadelphia

1928	France	United States	Paris
1929	France	United States	Paris
1930	France	United States	Paris
1931	France	Great Britain	Paris
1932	France	United States	Paris
1933	Great Britain	France	Paris
1934	Great Britain	United States	Wimbledon
1935	Great Britain	United States	Wimbledon
1936	Great Britain	Australia	Wimbledon
1937	United States	Great Britain	Wimbledon
1938	United States	Australia	Philadelphia
1939	Australia	United States	Philadelphia
1940	Not held		
1941	Not held		
1942	Not held		
1943	Not held		
1944	Not held		
1945	Not held		
1946	United States	Australia	Melbourne
1947	United States	Australia	New York
1948	United States	Australia	New York
1949	United States	Australia	New York
1950	Australia	United States	New York
1951	Australia	United States	Sydney
1952	Australia	United States	Adelaide
1953	Australia	United States	Melbourne
1954	United States	Australia	Sydney
1955	Australia	United States	New York
1956	Australia	United States	Adelaide
1957	Australia	United States	Melbourne
1958	United States	Australia	Brisbane
1959	Australia	United States	New York
1960	Australia	Italy	Sydney
1961	Australia	Italy	Melbourne

1962	Australia	Mexico	Brisbane
1963	United States	Australia	Adelaide
1964	Australia	United States	Cleveland
1965	Australia	Spain	Sydney
1966	Australia	India	Melbourne
1967	Australia	Spain	Brisbane
1968	United States	Australia	Adelaide
1969	United States	Romania	Cleveland
1970	United States	West Germany	Cleveland
1971	United States	Romania	Charlotte
1972	United States	Romania	Bucharest
1973	Australia	United States	Cleveland
1974	South Africa	India (Walkover)	
1975	Sweden	Czechoslovakia	Stockholm
1976	Italy	Chile	Santiago
1977	Australia	Italy	Sydney
1978	United States	Great Britain	Palm Springs
1979	United States	Italy	San Francisco
1980	Czechoslovakia	Italy	Prague
1981	United States	Argentina	Cincinnati
1982	United States	France	Grenoble
1983	Australia	Sweden	Melbourne
1984	Sweden	United States	Gothenburg
1985	Sweden	West Germany	Munich
1986	Australia	Sweden	Melbourne
1987	Sweden	India	Gothenburg
1988	W. Germany	Sweden	
1989	W. Germany	Sweden	

Davis Cup great

Nicola Pietrangeli played 163 Davis Cup rubbers for Italy, more than anyone in history. He won the most singles rubbers (78) and doubles rubbers (42) and the most rubbers overall (120) and also played in the most ties (66).

Davis, Dwight Filly

USA (1879-1945) — The donor of the Davis Cup, the trophy at stake in the international team championship. A Harvard undergraduate, he played against the British Isles in the first two matches of that competition, winning a single and partnering Holcombe Ward successfully in the doubles in 1900 and, with Ward again, losing to the Dohertys in the doubles in 1902.

Dead ball

A ball which has lost air pressure and consequently does not rebound as well as a normal or live ball. Poor stroke habits may result from using dead balls.

Deep-court game

A style of play in which the player stays deep or in the backcourt.

Deep shot

A term used to describe a shot that lands within the court near the baseline. A deep serve is one that lands within the service court near the service line.

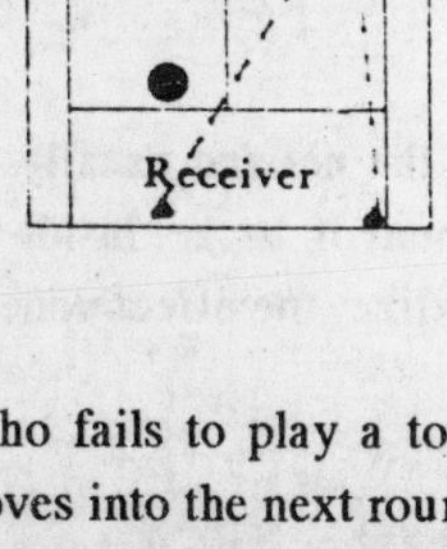

Default

A player who fails to play a tournament match loses by default; the opponent moves into the next round.

Defensive shot

A stroke made without any aggressive intent. Normally made when under pressure and often when the ball is well below the level of the net.

Defensive volley

A volleying stroke made from below the level of the net. Also called low volley.

Delivery

A service.

Deuce

If each player wins three points, the score in a game is deuce. After that, if they have both won an equal number of points, the score is again deuce.

Dewar Cup

The Dewar Cup, sponsored by the whiskey firm of Dewar, flourished from 1968 to 1976. It was an integrated circuit of British indoor tournaments staged in a continuous series of weeks in the autumn, each event being complete in itself but giving qualifying points for the climax. This was always staged in London, at the Crystal Palace in the first 2 years, subsequently at the Royal Albert Hall.

Die

Descriptive of a ball that scarcely bounces at all.

Dink

A medium to slow return hit low over the net and usually at an acute angle, but also at the feet of an opponent if he is inside the service court area. Used especially to neutralize the effectiveness of volleying attacks.

Dipping balls

Balls that barely clear the net, then drop fast and short.

Dirt courts

When firm, well-drained subsoil exists, stone or slag foundations are not necessary for inexpensive dirt courts. Remove topsoil and level subsoil by rolling and filling. Surface with at least a 2-inch covering of clay sand and salt as noted below. Subsoil should be raked prior to surfacing to bond the clay mixture to the direct foundation.

The advantages are low initial cost, ease under foot for the player, and medium fast ball bounce.

The disadvantages are the constant maintenance which such a court requires and the slow drying time after a rain.

Dod, Lottie

UK (1871-1940) — The youngest player ever to win the Wimbledon singles, Dod won first at the age of 15, in 1887. Her precocity had already been in evidence for some years. She won the women's doubles at Manchester when she was only 11, and at 14 she beat the reigning Wimbledon champion, Maud Wason, at Bath. In her first Wimbledon final she beat Blanche Bingley (later Mrs. Hillyard), who herself was to win the title six times. Dod was so athletic and had such good ball sense that the older woman was outclassed, 6-2, 6-0. She won four more times, then retired from tennis at the ripe old age of 21 to seek new challenges. She also won the Ladies' Open Golf Championship in 1904, and she also played hockey for England in 1899 and 1900.

Doherty, Reginald Frank

UK (1874-1910) — A more fluent but less powerful player than his younger brother Laurie, whom he preceded as the outstanding British player. Wimbledon champion 1897-1900; doubles 1897, 1898, 1899, 1900, 1901, 1903, 1904, 1905.

Double fault

When the server has served two serves out of bounds on the same point.

Double hit

A ball stroked twice on the same play — an illegal play.

Doubles

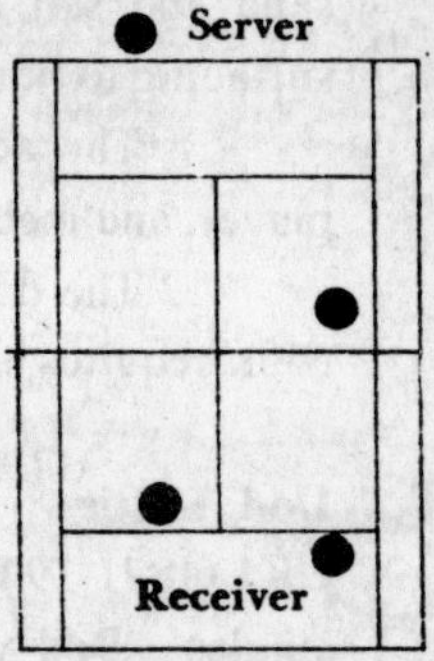

With the two extra players on court, the game of doubles can often provide a great deal of fun. The basic rules are in general the same as those for singles, but with a few exceptions. The court is wider and the service sidelines are now included, often referred to as the 'tramlines', (see plan of the court) thus giving more room in which to play the shots. The ball has to be hit alternately by one or other player of the opposing pairs. Occasionally you hear the clash of rackets when both players go

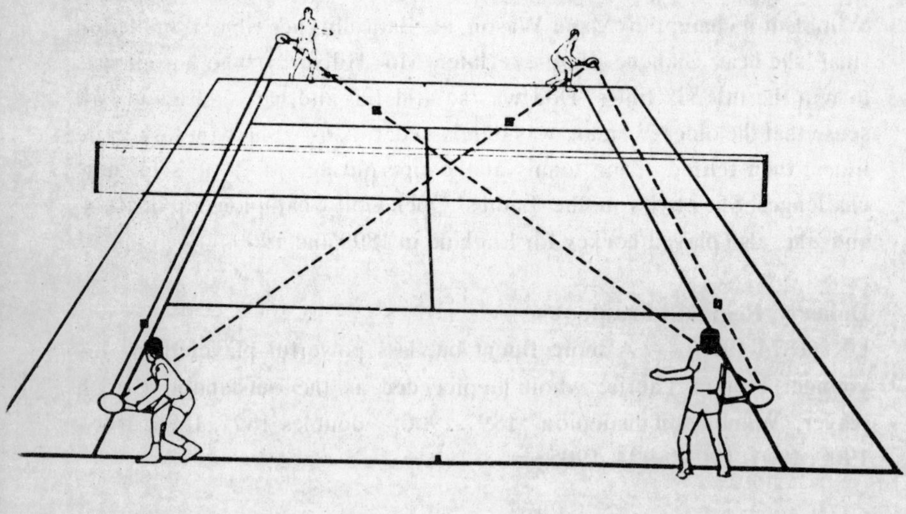

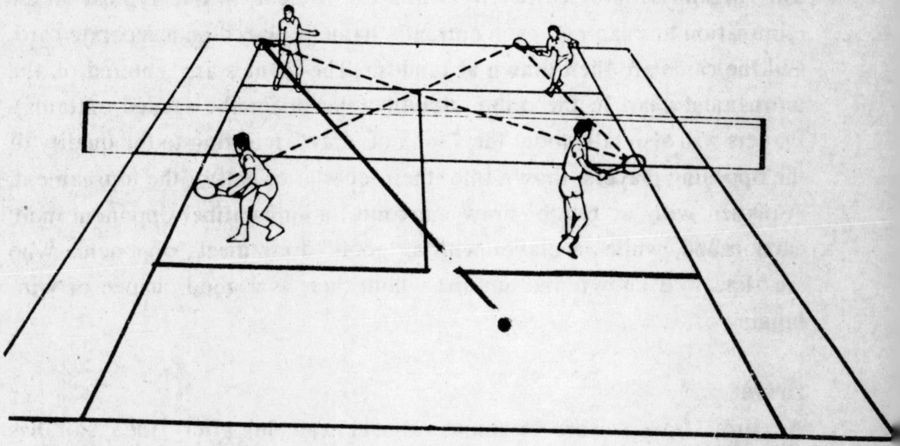

for the same ball, but this is better than that classic situation of both players leaving the ball and shouting 'yours'!

Double Elimination Tournament

A type of tournament in which a player must lose two matches before being eliminated from the tournament.

Doubles line

The outside sideline on a court—used in doubles only.

Down-the-line

A shot hit near a sideline which travels close to, and parallel to, the same from which the shot was initially hit.

Draft

The draw; the list of players entered for any event written out and bracketed in the order in which they are drawn to play.

Draw

The organization of competitors in a tournament; in the typical single elimination tournament, each entrant's name is placed on a separate card, and the cards are then drawn at random. The names are entered on the tournament chart in the order drawn (except for the seeded entrants). Players will also talk about the "luck of draw" referring to the quality of the opposing players drawn into their quarter or half of the tournament. A player with a "tough" draw must meet a high-caliber opponent in an early round, while a player with a "good" draw meets opponents who are less well known and against whom there is a good chance of winning.

Drive

A firm stroke, either forehand or backhand, hit after the ball has bounced.

Drive volley

A hard-hit volleying stroke, either by forehand or backhand.

Drobny, Jaroslav

Czechoslovakia (born 1921) — Exiled himself from Czechoslovakia in 1949, became an Egyptian subject in 1950 and a naturalized Briton in 1960. One of the great post-war clay court competitors with tremendous left-hand serve and smash, and delicate touch, he played in some of Wimbledon's most dramatic and emotional matches and eventually won the singles in 1954 at the age of 33. He played in 43 Davis Cup rubbers, and won 37.

Drop

The unnatural down curve of a ball when hit with a "lifting" stroke that gives a top curl or forward spin.

Drop shot

A soft shot which lands close to the net and bounces low.

Drop volley

A volleying stroke hit softly and easily just over the net.

Du Pont, Margaret

USA (born 1918) — One of the Americans who made the United States invincible in the women's game in the years following World War II. A splendid all-rounder but particularly noteworthy for her prowess as a doubles player. Her first Wimbledon success was in 1947, her last, the mixed doubles with Neale Fraser in 1962.

Drysdale, E. Clifford

S. Africa (born 1941) — Basically right-handed with a two-handed backhand and an occasional two-handed forehand.

Dubler Cup

An international competition for men run by the Veteran International Tennis Association in much the same way as the Davis Cup. The competition began in 1958 when Italy won.

Duffer

A poor player.

Durr, Francoise

France (born 1942) — Now Mrs. Browning. The outstanding French woman player of the 1960s and 1970s. Shrewd and unorthodox, particularly in her serve and on the backhand, she excelled in doubles. She gained her major singles successes in 1967 when she won the French and German titles and reached the US semi-finals, but in doubles won a host of titles with a variety of partners, including five successive French victories.

E

Earned point
A point won through skilful play rather than through an opponent's unforced mistake.

Eastern forehand grip
An easy way to learn how to hold a racket correctly for a forehand stroke is to place the racket on flat surface like a desk or table. Now

balance the racket on its edge so the strings are not face down on the flat surface.

Echelon formation
A positioning of players in a doubles game in which one player stands close to the net and his partner plays deep.

Edberg, Stefan
Sweden (born 1966) — 1989-90 could have been the finest year of his career. Playing serene serve-volley tennis, he reached the French Open final on clay, with Wimbledon to follow on his favourite surface,

grass. Only Ivan Lendl in the last five years has attained the finals of both events. But such is the difference between reaching finals and winning them; Edberg lost both and instead of enjoying his best year, has had his leanest, with just one title won in 1989. He won Wimbledon in 1988, 1990 and Australian championships in 1985, 1987.

Eighth point

Game or deuce (after deuce is reached), one player must win two points in a row to the game.

Elbow

'Getting the elbow' means tightening up under pressure. Tennis elbow is a painful physical condition.

Emerson, Roy

Australia (born 1936) — An athletic and persistent player and valuable asset to the Australia in the Davis Cup in 18 ties including 9 successive Challenge Rounds 1959 to 1967. Wimbledon champion 1964, 1965; doubles 1959, 1961. He holds a record six Australian titles, two US Championships, two Wimbledons and two French singles. Roy has the titles to prove it, having won two Italian doubles, a Canadian, three Wimbledons, six French and four US titles.

Error

A mistake made by a player during competition.

Even court

The right court since, whenever play is started in this court, an even number of points has been played in the current game.

Event

Any complete competition on the programme of a tournament.

Evert, Chris

USA (born 1954) — The phrase "grace under pressure" could have been invented for Chris Evert. The attractive Floridian has handled the pressure atop women's tennis for nearly 20 years with relentless concentration and an ageless, clean-hitting style of play. She was still 15 when she beat the reigning Grand Slam champion, Margaret Court, at a tournament in Charlotte, North Carolina, in September 1970. The following year, as a surprise selection, she won both her Wightman Cup rubbers against vastly more experienced players, and she reached the semi-finals of the US Open at her first attempt. She quickly established herself as one of the top four players in the world, and her Wimbledon debut was greeted with more media attention than anyone since Maureen Connoly, with whom she was inevitably compared.

An icon among Americans, she has been married twice: to the British player John Lloyd from 1979 to 1987, and to American skier Andy Mill from July 1988.

Best Wins:-

Wimbledon	1974, 1976, 1981
French Open	1974, 1975, 1979, 1980, 1983, 1985, 1986
US Open	1975, 1976, 1977, 1978, 1980, 1982
Australian Open	1982, 1984
Italian Open	1974, 1975, 1980, 1981, 1982,
Canadian Open	1974, 1980, 1984, 1985
German Open	1983, 1985

F

Face
Either side of the striking surface (strings) of a racket.

Face of racket
The hitting surface of the racket.

Falkenburg, Robert
USA (born 1926) — Won the US Junior Championship in 1943-44 and came to Europe in 1947 with the reputation of possessing the fastest service in the US. He won at Queen's Club, but lost to Pails in quarter-final at Wimbledon and then won the doubles with Kramer, defeating Mottram and Sidwell in final.

Falls
Dies; the second bound of a ball in play, or its first bound if out of court.

Fast court
A court on which fairly hard hit balls lose a minimum of pace when bouncing, normally low.

Fast-dry tennis courts
Fast-Drying tennis courts have a specially prepared surface mixture which is basically crushed burnt brick or crushed green stone, ground and screened and mixed with a chemical binder. During processing special chemical binders are used to assure firmness.

Fault

A serve which goes out of court or into the net.

Federation Cup

The women's equivalent of the Davis Cup. Instituted in 1963 by the International Lawn Tennis Federation as the women's team championship of the world.

Winners

1963	USA
1964	Australia
1965	Australia
1966	USA
1967	USA
1968	Australia
1969	USA
1970	Australia
1971	Australia
1972	South Africa
1973	Australia
1974	Australia
1975	Czechoslovakia
1976	USA
1977	USA
1978	USA
1979	USA
1980	USA
1981	USA
1982	USA
1983	Czechoslovakia
1984	Czechoslovakia
1985	Czechoslovakia
1986	USA
1987	W. Germany
1988	Czechoslovakia
1989	USA

Feeder stroke
A drop-and-hit swing used in practising or to return a ball to the server after a point.

Fifteen
In traditional scoring, the first point scored by a player or pair.

Fifteen-all
The score when each player has scored one point.

Fifteen-(thirty-love, or forty-love)
The score when the server has won one (fifteen), two (thirty), or three (forty) points and the opponent none.

Fifth point
Game, 40-30, 30-40.

Final round
The last round, in which the two surviving players or teams are opposed to each other; commonly referred to as the "finals".

Finishing shot
A shot which cannot be returned by the opponent.

Finland
Lawn Tennis Association of Finland was founded in April 1911 with five lawn tennis clubs, two with covered courts. The first official lawn tennis championship in Finland were played in Hango (Hanko) in 1912 for the Nordic Cup (an annual competition).

First point
15-love or love-15.

Flat

Flat face is a term used to describe the position of the racket head when the face is perpendicular to the court and faces the net squarely, sometimes called a square face. A flat drive is produced with a flat face and a level swing, thus directing the ball in a fairly straight trajectory with little arc and little or no spin.

Flat service

A serve delivered without spin.

Flat shot

A ball hit in such a manner as not to rotate when travelling through the air.

Flub

To miss an easy shot.

Fluke

A slang expression meaning an accidental return, or one that was intended in some other way. Also, the victory of a poorer player over a stronger player, through chance or luck; an "upset".

Flushing meadow

New York home of the US Open.

Follow through

The continuation of a stroke after impact with the ball.

Foot fault

Illegal foot movement before service that is penalized by the loss of that particular serve. Common foot faults are: stepping on or ahead of the baseline before the ball has been contacted; and running along the baseline before serving.

FOOT FAULT

Footwear

Special shoes, designed solely for the game, have been worn by tennis players since early days at Wimbledon.

Footwork

The action of the feet in moving into position to play a shot. Correct footwork is essential for proper balance and effective grooving of strokes.

Forced error

An error made by a player when the quality of the opponent's shot is such that his chances of returning the ball into court are minimal.

Forcing shot

A shot or series of shots that keep the opponent on the defensive or out of position.

Forecourt

The area of the court between the service line and the net.

Forehand

A stroke made on the right side of a right-handed player or on the left side of a left-hander. So called because the palm of the hand is towards the net.

Forehand Drive

Forehand drive

The player should hold the racket at the ready, with his arms slightly bent, but relaxed, in front of him, steadying the racket with his left hand, so that his right hand can get a grip on it quite easily (forehand Eastern grip). The knees should be bent slightly. Watch the ball. Both hands should be close to the body. This is known as the position of readiness. The upper part of the body should start to twist.

Fork

An iron upright struck in the ground at the centre of the court to keep the net at exactly the required height.

Form

The style in which a player carries him and makes his strokes. Also, his playing skill.

Foro Italico

The site of the Italian championships in Rome.

Forth point

Game, 30-30, 15-40, or 40-15.

Forty

Three points scored for either player.

Forward impulse

The straight forward portion of the swing of any shot.

Forward spin

A forward rotation of the ball in the direction of its flight. Opposite of backspin.

Forward swing

The motion of the racket toward and through the ball.

Frame

The rim of the racket head plus the handle of the racket.

France

The French, as masters of real tennis, quickly profited from the idea of adapting the old game to outdoor conditions and within 20 years of the invention of lawn tennis both Paris and the Riviera were major international centres of the game. Unable to grow grass of the right quality for competition, the French concentrated on the development of clay courts—terre battue—and the fine sand of the Rivera became recognized as an almost perfect surface for the game.

The origins of lawn tennis in France are a little obscure. The first clubs were certainly founded by Englishmen but there is disagreement about who they were.

The first championships in France were held in 1891 (men's singles and men's doubles). From 1925 entries have been accepted from all countries. Held on the courts of the famous Stade Roland Garros, at Auteuil, this championship is regarded as the leading hard court event.

Fraser, Neale Nanrew

Australia (born 1933) — A consistently aggressive left-hander, with a plain, direct serve and volley game, he was trained by Hopman, winning 18 of 21 Davis Cup rubbers between 1958 and 1963, and later captained the Australian team which recaptured the trophy at Cleveland in 1973 and at Melbourne in 1978 and 1983. He won the US singles 1959/60 and doubles 1957/59/60, the French doubles 1958/60/62, and Australian doubles 1957/58/62.

French Championships

The French Championships were first held in 1891 but they remained 'closed', open only to members of French Clubs, until 1925 when they became a fully international event.

Men's Singles

1925	R. Lacoste	FRA
1926	H. Cochet	FRA
1927	R. Lacoste	FRA
1928	H. Cochet	FRA
1929	R. Lacoste	FRA
1930	H. Cochet	FRA
1931	J. Borotra	FRA
1932	H. Cochet	FRA
1933	J.H. Crawford	AUS
1934	G. von Cramm	GER
1935	F.J. Perry	UK
1936	G. von Cramm	GER
1937	H. Henkel	GER
1938	J.D. Budge	USA
1939	W.D. McNeill	USA
1940	Not held	
1941	Not held	
1942	Not held	
1943	Not held	
1944	Not held	
1945	Not held	
1946	M. Barnard	FRA
1947	J. Asboth	HUN
1948	F.A. Parker	USA
1949	F.A. Parker	USA
1950	J.E. Patty	USA
1951	J. Drobny	EG
1952	J. Drobny	EG
1953	K.R. Rosewall	AUS
1954	M.A. Trabert	USA
1955	M.A. Trabert	USA
1956	L.A. Hoad	AUS
1957	S. Davidson	SWE

1958	M.G. Rose	AUS
1959	N. Pietrangeli	ITA
1960	N. Pietrangeli	ITA
1961	M. Santana	SPA
1962	R.G. Laver	AUS
1963	R.S. Emerson	AUS
1964	M. Santana	SPA
1965	F.S. Stolle	AUS
1966	A.D. Roche	AUS
1967	R.S. Emerson	AUS
1968	K.R. Rosewall	AUS
1969	R.G. Laver	AUS
1970	J. Kodes	CZ
1971	J. Kodes	CZ
1972	A. Gimeno	SPA
1973	I. Nastase	ROM
1974	B. Borg	SWE
1975	B. Borg	SWE
1976	A. Panatta	ITA
1977	G. Vilas	ARG
1978	B. Borg	SWE
1979	B. Borg	SWE
1980	B. Borg	SWE
1981	B. Borg	SWE
1982	M. Wilander	SWE
1983	Y. Noah	FRA
1984	I. Lendl	CZ
1985	M. Wilander	SWE
1986	I. Lendl	CZ
1987	I. Lendl	CZ
1988	M. Wilander	SWE
1989	Michael Chang	USA
1990	Andreus Gomez	ECU

Women's Singles

1925	S. Lenglen	FRA
1926	S. Lenglen	FRA
1927	K. Bouman	NETH
1928	H.N. Wills	USA
1929	H.N. Wills	USA
1930	H.N. Moody	USA
1931	C. Aussem	GER
1932	H.N. Moody	USA
1933	M.C. Scriven	UK
1934	M.C. Scriven	UK
1935	H. Sperling	DEN
1936	H. Sperling	DEN
1937	H. Sperling	DEN
1938	S. Mathieu	FRA
1939	S. Mathieu	FRA
1940	Not held	
1941	Not held	
1942	Not held	
1943	Not held	
1944	Not held	
1945	Not held	
1946	M.E. Osborne	USA
1947	P.C. Todd	USA
1948	N. Landry	FRA
1949	M.E. du Pont	USA
1950	D.J. Hart	USA
1951	S.J. Fry	USA
1952	D.J. Hart	USA
1953	M.C. Connolly	USA
1954	M.C. Connolly	USA
1955	A. Mortimer	UK
1956	A. Gibson	USA
1957	S.J. Bloomer	UK

1958	S. Kormoczy	HUN
1959	C.C. Truman	UK
1960	D.R. Hard	USA
1961	A.S. Haydon	UK
1962	M. Smith	AUS
1963	L.R. Turner	AUS
1964	M. Smith	AUS
1965	L.R. Turner	AUS
1966	A.S. Jones	UK
1967	F. Durr	FRA
1968	N. Richey	USA
1969	M. Court	AUS
1970	M. Court	AUS
1971	E.F. Goolagong	AUS
1972	B.J. King	USA
1973	M. Court	AUS
1974	C.M. Evert	USA
1975	C.M. Evert	USA
1976	S. Barker	UK
1977	M. Jansovec	YUG
1978	V. Ruzici	ROM
1979	C. Lloyd	USA
1980	C. Lloyd	USA
1981	H. Mandlikova	CZ
1982	M. Navratilova	USA
1983	C. Lloyd	USA
1984	M. Navratilova	USA
1985	C. Lloyd	USA
1986	C. Lloyd	USA
1987	S. Graf	W.GER
1988	S. Graf	W.GER
1989	Arantxa Sanchez	SPA
1990	Monica Seles	Yug

Men's Doubles

1946	Marcel Bernard, Yvon Petra	FRA
1947	Eustace Fannin, Eric Sturgess	SAF
1948	Lennart Bergelin (SWE), Jaroslav Drobny	CZ
1949	Richard Gonzales, Frank Parker	USA
1950	William Talbert, Tony Trabert	USA
1951	Ken McGregor, Frank Sedgman	AUS
1952	Ken McGregor, Frank Sedgman	AUS
1953	Lew Hoad, Ken Rosewall	AUS
1954	Vic Seixas, Tony Trabert	USA
1955	Vic Seixas, Tony Trabert	USA
1956	Don Candy (Aus), Robert Perry	USA
1957	Mal Anderson, Ashley Cooper	AUS
1958	Ashley Cooper, Neale Fraser	AUS
1959	Nicola Pietrangeli, Orlando Sirola	ITA
1960	Roy Emerson, Neale Fraser	AUS
1961	Roy Emerson, Rod Laver	AUS
1962	Roy Emerson, Neale Fraser	AUS
1963	Roy Emerson (Aus), Manuel Santana	SPA
1964	Roy Emerson, Ken Fletcher	AUS
1965	Roy Emerson, Fred Stolle	AUS
1966	Clark Graebner, Dennis Ralston	USA
1967	John Newcombe, Tony Roche	AUS
1968	Ken Rosewall, Fred Stolle	AUS
1969	John Newcombe, Tony Roche	AUS
1970	Ilie Nastase, Ion Tiriac	ROM
1971	Arthur Ashe, Marty Riessen	USA
1972	Bob Hewitt, Frew McMillan	SAF
1973	John Newcombe (Aus), Tom Okker	HOL
1974	Dick Crealy (Aus), Onny Parun	NZ
1975	Brian Gottfried (USA), Raul Ramirez	MEX
1976	Fred Mcnair, Sherwood Stewart	USA
1977	Brian Gottfried (USA), Raul Ramirez	MEX
1978	Gene Mayer, Hank Pfister	USA

1979	Sandy Mayer, Gene Mayer	USA
1980	Victor Amaya, Hank Pfister	USA
1981	Heinz Gunthardt (Swi), Balazs Troczy	HUN
1982	Sherwood Stewart, Ferdi Taygan	USA
1983	Anders Jarryd, Hans Simonsson	SWE
1984	Henri Leconte, Yannick Noah	FRA
1985	Mark Edmondson, Kim Warwick	AUS
1986	John Fitzgerald (Aus), Tomas Smid	CZ
1987	Andres Fitzgerald (Aus), Tomas Smid	CZ
1988	Andres Gomez (Ecu), Emilio Sanchez	SPA
1989	Jim Grabb, Patrick McEnroe	USA
1990	Sergio Casal, Emilio Sanchez	SPA

Women's Doubles

1946	Louise Brough, Margaret Osborne	USA
1947	Louise Brough, Margaret Osborne	USA
1948	Doris Hart, Pat Todd	USA
1949	Louise Brough, Margaret Du Pont (nee Osborne)	USA
1950	Shirley Fry, Doris Hart	USA
1951	Shirely Fry, Doris Hart	USA
1952	Shirely Fry, Doris Hart	USA
1953	Shirely Fry, Doris Hart	USA
1954	Maureen Connolly (USA), Nell Hopman	AUS
1955	Beverley Fleitz, Darlene Hard	USA
1956	Angela Buxton (UK), Althea Gibson	USA
1957	Shirley Bloomer (UK), Darlene Hard	USA
1958	Yola Ramirez, Rosa Reyes	MEX
1959	Sandra Reynolds, Renee Schuurman	SAF
1960	Maria Bueno (Bra), Darlene Hard	USA
1961	Sandra Reynolds, Renee Schuurman	SAF
1962	Sandra Price (nee Reynolds), Renee Schuurman	SAF
1963	Ann Jones (UK), Renee Schuurman	SAF
1964	Margaret Smith, Lesley Turner	AUS
1965	Margaret Smith, Lesley Turner	AUS

1966 Margaret Smith, Judy Tegart AUS
1967 Francoise Durr (Fra), Gail Sheriff AUS
1968 Francoise Durr (Fra), Ann Jones UK
1969 Francoise Durr (Fra), Ann Jones UK
1970 Francoise Durr, Gail Chanfreau FRA
1971 Francoise Furr, Gail Chanfreau FRA
1972 Billie Jean King (USA), Betty Stove HOL
1973 Margaret Court (Aus), Virginia Wade UK
1974 Chris Evert (USA), Olga Morozova USSR
1975 Chris Evert (USA), Martina Navratilova CZ
1976 Fiorella Bonicelli (Uru), Gail Lovera FRA
1977 Regina Marsikova (CS), Pam Teeguarden USA
1978 Mimi Jausovec (Yug), Virginia Ruzici ROM
1979 Betty Stove (Hol), Wendy Turnbull AUS
1980 Kathy Jordan, Anne Smith USA
1981 Ros Fairbank, Tanya Harford SAF
1982 Martina Navratilova, Anne Smith USA
1983 Ros Fairbank (S.Af), Candy Reynolds USA
1984 Martina Novratilova, Pam Shriver USA
1985 Martina Novratilova, Pam Shriver USA
1986 Martina Navratilova (USA), Andrea Temesvari HUN
1987 Martina Navratilova, Pam Shriver USA
1988 Martina Navratilova, Pam Shriver USA
1989 Larissa Savchenko, Natalya Zvereva USSR
1990 Jana Novotna, Helena Sukova CZ

Mixed Doubles

1925 J. Brugnon, S. Lenglen (Fra)
1926 J. Brugnon, S. Lenglen (Fra)
1927 J. Borotra, M. Bordes (Fra)
1928 H. Cochet (Fra), E. Bennett (UK)
1929 H. Cochet (Fra), E. Bennett (UK)
1930 W. T. Tilen (USA), C. Aussem (Ger)
1931 P.D.B. Spence (SA), B. Nuthall (UK)

1932 F.J. Perry, B. Nuthall (UK)
1933 J. H. Carwford (Aus), M. C. Scriven (UK)
1934 J. Borotra, C. Rosambert (Fra)
1935 M. Bernard (Fra), L. Payot (Swi)
1936 M. Bernard (Fra), A.M. Yorke (UK)
1937 Y. Petra, S. Mathieu (Fra)
1938 D. Mitic (Yug), S. Mathieu (Fra)
1939 E.T. Cooke, S. Fabyan (USA)
1940 Not held
1941 Not held
1942 Not held
1943 Not held
1944 Not held
1945 Not held
1946 Budge Patty, Pauline Betz (USA)
1947 Eric Sturgess, Sheila Summers (SAf)
1948 Jaroslav Drobny (Cz), Pat Todd (USA)
1949 Eric Sturgess, Sheila Summers S.AF
1950 Enrique Morea (Arg), Barbara Scofield (USA)
1951 Frank Sedgman (Aus), Doris Hart (USA)
1952 Frank Sedgman (Aus), Doris Hart (USA)
1953 Vic Seixas, Doris Hart (USA)
1954 Lew Hoad (Aus), Maureen Connolly (USA)
1955 Gordon Forbes (SAf), Darlene Hard (USA)
1956 Luis Ayala (Chl), Thelma Long (AUS)
1957 Jan Javorsky, Vera Puzejova (Cz)
1958 Nicola Pietrangeli (Ita)
1959 Billy Knight (UK), Yola Ramirez (Mex)
1960 Bob Howe (Aus), Maria Bueno (Bra)
1961 Rod Laver (Aus), Darlene Hard (USA)
1962 Bob Howe (Aus), Renee Schuurman (SAf)
1963 Ken Fletcher, Margaret Smith (Aus)
1964 Ken Fletcher, Margaret Smith (Aus)
1965 Ken Fletcher, Margaret Smith (Aus)

1966 Frew McMillan, Annette Van Zyl (S Af)
1967 Owen Davidson (Aus), Billie Jean King (USA)
1968 Jean-Claude Barclay, Francoise Durr (Fra)
1969 Marty Riessen (USA), Margaret Court (Aus)
1970 Bob Hewitt (SAf), Billie Jean King (USA)
1971 Jean-Claude Barclay, Francoise Durr (Fra)
1972 Kim Warwick, Evonne Goolagong (Aus)
1973 Jean-Claude Barclay, Francoise Durr (Fra)
1974 Ivan Molina (Col), Martina Navratilova (Cz)
1975 Thomaz Koch (Bra), Fiorella Bonicelli (Uru)
1976 Kim Warwick (Aus), Ilana Kloss (SAf)
1977 John McEnroe, Mary Carillo (USA)
1978 Pavel Slozil, Renata Tomanova (Cz)
1979 Bob Hewitt (S Af), Wendy Turnbull (Aus)
1980 Bill Martin, Anne Smith (USA)
1981 Jimmy Arias, Andrea Jaeger (USA)
1982 John Lloyd (UK), Wendy Turnbull (Aus)
1983 E. Teltscher, B.S. Jordan (USA)
1984 R.L. Stocktonn, A.E. Smith (USA)
1985 H.P. Guenthardt (Swi), M. Navratilova (USA)
1986 K. Flach, K. Jordan (USA)
1987 E. Sanchez (Spa), Pam Shriver (USA)
1988 J. Lozano (Mex), L. McNeil (USA)

Fromholtz, Dianne

Australia (born 1956) — Reckoned to be the finest left-handed woman player ever produced by Australia, the attractive Dianne has lost her sparkle after being ranked world No 4 in 1979. She entered the world top 10 in 1976 and in 1979 earned more than 1,00,000 pound in prize money.

Fry, Shirley J.

USA (born 1927) — Dominated by the exceptional standards of her rival Americans like Margaret du Pont, Louise Brough, Doris Hart and

Maureen Connolly she served a long apprenticeship before becoming Wimbledon champion in 1956. Having first challenged in 1948 she had been beaten in the quarter-final three times, in the semi-final twice and in the final, once—on each occasion by a fellow American. She and Doris Hart won the Wimbledon doubles three years in succession, the third time, 1953, for the total loss of only 4 games. In that year they won the final from Maureen Connolly and Julia Sampson by 6-0, 6-0.

Full stroke

Any stroke in which the player swings arm, racket and body to the fullest extent possible.

G

Galea Cup

International team championship for men under 21. Match format four singles among two players, one doubles. First held in 1950.

Gallery

The spectators watching any game or match.

Gallery play

A slang expression meaning fancy strokes made for the purpose of attracting the attention of the spectators, or a spectacular stroke made in the regular course of a game.

Game

A player has won a game by winning four points before his opponent and holding a minimum two-point lead.

Game point

The point which, if won, wins the game.

Games-all

The score of a set when the games are even at five-all, six-all, or higher. Same as "deuce" in the score of a set.

Game score

Points are reckoned as "15", "30", "40" and "game" rather than "1", "2", "3", and "4". A player must win a game by at least two points. Therefore, if each player has three points, the score is called "deuce" or

"40-40" or "40-all". The player who wins the next point has "advantage" (not "50-40"). If he loses the next point, the score goes back to deuce.

Garrison, Zina

USA (born 1963) — In 1981 she received the International Tennis Federation's Junior of the Year award after winning the junior titles at Wimbledon and the US Open. Bold, adventurous and mobile she has the ability to please crowds as well as win matches.

Germany

Germany was the sixth country to challenge in the Davis Cup and, since the Austrians did not appear on court, the fifth to play in the competition. From 1913, when Germany beat France in the first round and lost to the USA, they fielded strong teams. German players enjoyed some early success at Wimbledon. Dreuzer (1907 and 1913) reached the quarter-finals of the all-comers' singles, Rahe was a semi-finalist in 1909 and 1911.

German Championships

The German Championships, staged from 1892 in Hamburg, are older than the game as an organised sport, preceding by some 10 years the formation of the Deutscher Lawn Tennis Bund. In 1979 the women's events were staged as a separate tournament in Berlin. This entailed an interruption for 1980 when priority was given to the staging of the Federation Cup.

Gibson, Althea

USA (born 1927) — Now Mrs. Darbin. The first black player to dominate international lawn tennis, relying on fierce serving and considerable strength and reach. Won Wimbledon singles 1957/58 and doubles (with Angela Buxton) 1957 and (with Maria Bueno) 1958.

Gonzales, Richardo

USA (born 1928) — This big Californian, Mexican by race, was to a great extent the dominant figure in lawn tennis in the 1950s and much of the 1960s. He became a contracted professional in 1949 and thus for the most fruitful part of his career was not seen on the courts staging the traditionally major events. He wielded a shattering service and the whole pattern of his game was of overwhelming strength. Best world ranking No. 1 in 1949.

Good ball

A general term applied to any ball which lands in the proper playing area.

Goolagong, Evonne Fay

Australia (born 1951) — Now Mrs. Roger Cawley (married in 1975). One of the naturally gifted of champions, she was the first of her aborigin race to excel at the game. Suddenly in 1971 at the age of 19, three years before her coach Vic. Edwards had forecast she would, she swept through both the French Championships and Wimbledon on a cloud of inspiration to win her first major titles. Although she reached the Wimbledon final again the following year and twice more, in 1975 and 1976, it was not until 1980 that she won again — four years after the birth of her daughter, Kelly.

Gore, Arthur Wentworth

UK (1868-1928) — Perhaps the greatest stalwart of the British game. He first competed at Wimbledon in 1888. Between then and 1927 he never missed a meeting in 40 years. He won the singles in 1901 and for the third time in 1909 when he was 41 years old. Wimbledon champion 1901, 1908, 1909; doubles 1909.

Gore, Spencer W.

UK (1850-1906) — He won Wimbledon men's singles in 1877. The very first champion, though he wrote scathingly about the merits of lawn tennis as compared with real tennis or rackets.

Gottfried, Brian

USA (born 1952) — He became one of a group of only 20 players with similar credentials since the rankings were started in 1885. He was runner-up in the French Open in 1977 and a Wimbledon semi-finalist in 1980 — Brian's career earnings of nearly $3m emphasize his match-winning ability.

Graf, Steffi

W. Germany (born 1969) — In 1984, a leggy, tousle-haired 15-year-old mite named Steffi Graf travelled to Kooyong to compete in the Australian Open. She lost third round to veteran Wendy Turnbull. Few imagined back then that in the short space of three years, Steffi was to become the future of women's tennis. In the three years from January 1986 to the beginning of 1989, Graf has won 95 per cent of her matches; 212 wins 11 losses. Such is her technical superiority — her great power, speed and consistency - to say nothing of her concentration and fighting qualities, that experts predict she has the women's game at her mercy for as long as she's interested. Graf had not reached her 18th birthday when she joined the Million Dollar Club in 1987. Two months later she was crowned the youngest-ever French Open champion, defeating Martina Navratilova 8-6 in the third set for her first Grand Slam title. There was no stopping her in 1988 as she rolled through the first traditional Grand Slam in 18 years, adding an Olympic gold medal for good measure. She won Wimbledon in 1988, 1989; US Open 1988, 1989; French Open 1987, 1988; Australian championship 1988, 1990.

Grand Prix

A linked series of men's tournaments held between January and December and embracing all the major championships.

Grand Slam

Winning the four leading championships (Wimbledon, US, French and Australian) in a year. The following players have achieved this feat: (Single years indicates all four titles won in one year)

Men's Singles

Donald Budge (USA)	1938
Rod Laver (Aus)	1962
Rod Laver (Aus)	1969

Women's Singles

Maureen Connolly (USA)	1952, 1953
Margaret Court (Aus)	1969, 1970, 1971
Martina Navratilova (USA	1983
Steffi Graf (W. Ger)	1988, 1989

Men's Doubles

Frank Sedgman (Aus)	1950, 1951, 1952
Ken McGregor (Aus)	1951, 1952

Women's Doubles

Louise Brough (USA)	1949
Maria Bueno (Bra)	1960
Martina Navratilova (USA)	1983, 1984, 1985, 1986, 1987
Pam Shriver (USA)	1983, 1984, 1985, 1986

Mixed Doubles

Margaret Smith (Aus)	1962, 1963, 1964
Ken Fletcher (Aus)	1963, 1964
Owen Davidson (Aus)	1966, 1967
Billie Jean King (USA)	1967

Grass courts

Grass courts in good condition provide one of the most luxurious of all surfaces. Until recently the Australian championships, Wimbledon matches, and many major U.S. tournaments have been held on grass and account for the term "Lawn Tennis". Grass provides great resilience underfoot and is a cool, clean surface, free of dust and glare. However, due to climate and soil requirements, it cannot be grown everywhere. The installation cost of a good grass court is high and daily care is required to keep it in playable condition.

Grass roots scheme

Term applied in Britain to the launching and development of the complete beginner. After looking for financial backing for some ten years, the Lawn Tennis Association of Great Britain, with the help of Green shield, started in 1970 a training scheme at grass-roots level with a pilot project in northwest England.

Great Britain

As (with Ireland) the British Isles, a founder member of the International Lawn Tennis Federation.

Grips

The importance of a proper grip cannot be stressed enough. There may be adjustments made in a player's swing, but a proper grip will last a player for a lifetime.

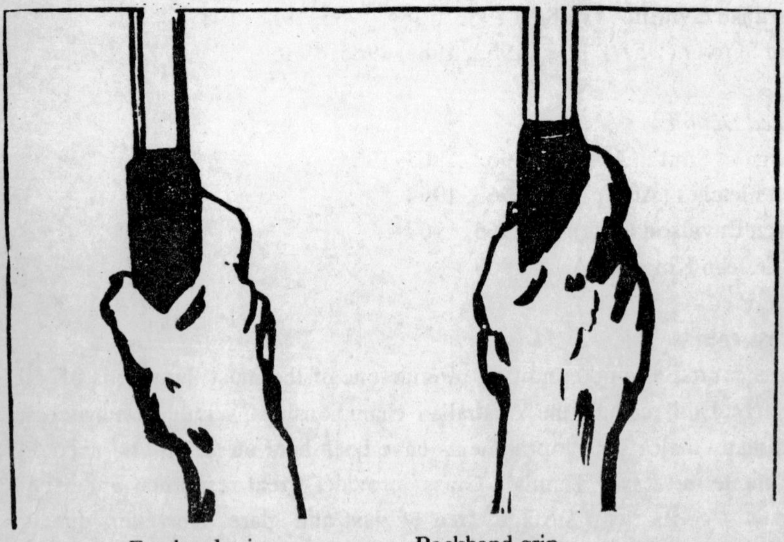

Forehand grip Backhand grip

Special names have been given to the forehand grips, based upon the position of the palm against the racket handle.

The backhand grip advocated in this chapter is the Eastern backhand grip. This is attained by putting the palm on the top of the racket, the knuckle of the index finger rides the top right ridge, and the thumb can be placed either behind the racket or underneath. This grip position provides the most stability and requires the least amount of wrist adjustment in order to provide a vertical racket head at impact.

Grip of racket
That portion of the racket which is grasped in the player's hand.

Grooved stroke
A stroke with which the player is so familiar that he performs it automatically.

Ground stroke
A shot hit after the ball has bounced.

Gut
An animal product (generally from lambs or hogs) often used to string tennis rackets.

Guy-rope
The rope stays used to support the poles between which the net is suspended.

H

Hack
To make a clumsy swing at a ball.

Hacker
Player whose strength lies in running down the opponent's shots and scraping the ball back, mostly soft and high and usually unstylishly.

Half-court line
The line dividing the service court into halves and separating the right and left service courts. Same as a centre service line.

Half-volley
A "pick-up" shot hit just after the bounce.

Handicap
Odds given or owed to a poorer player to equalize skill. Also, an event or match in which odds are assigned to unequal players, in order to equalize the chances of winning.

Handle
The end of the racket by which it is held.

Hard, Darlene, R.
USA (born 1936) — A formidable volleyer and doubles player and singles finalist at Wimbledon in 1959. Her most noted doubles partnership was with Maria Bueno. Became a coaching professional in 1963. Wimbledon champion (doubles) 1957, 1959, 1960, 1963; (mixed doubles) 1957, 1959, 1960.

Hart, Doris

USA (born 1925) — In spite of childhood illness which impeded her movement, she became one of the subtlest and most graceful of post-war competitors. Won Wimbledon singles 1951, doubles (with Pat Todd) 1947 and (with Shirley Fry) 1951/52/53/54.

Hartley, Canon John T.

UK (1849-1935) — The third Wimbledon champion and the first successfully to defend his title in 1880. But he was overwhelmed 6-0, 6-2, 6-1 the following year by the redoubtable William Renshaw. He was a graduate from the old game of real tennis and, like the two previous Wimbledon champions, Spencer Gore and Hadow, an old Harrovian. He was a little put out by getting so far in 1879 since as a clergyman with a living in Yorkshire, he had made no provision for the Sunday duties. Wimbledon champion, singles 1879, 1880.

Head

The oval part of a racket which carries the strings.

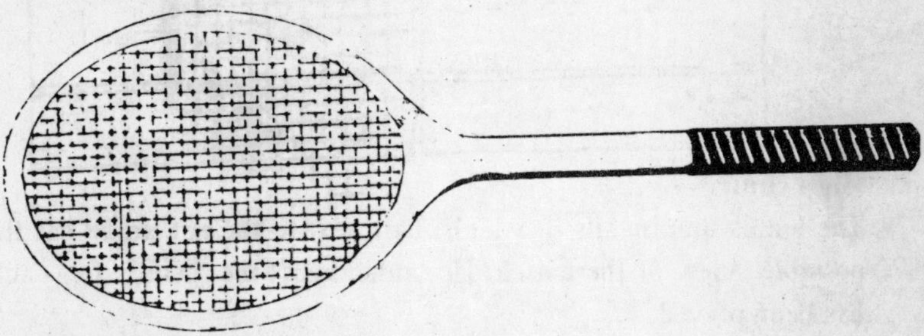

Hewitt, Robert Anthony John

South Africa (born 1940) — A big brooding volcano of a man, he had deceptively fine touch and became one of the greatest right-court returners of the serve of modern times. He enjoyed two careers — first with fellow Australian Fred Stolle and then with South Africa's Frew McMillan. He represented South Africa in Davis Cup 1964-74 and was a member of the successful team of 1974 that won by default from India.

High chair

The tennis umpire sits in a high chair next to the net, so he has the best possible view of the match. He announces the score after each point has been played.

History

For the tennis-player imbued with the antiquarian spirit, the early history of this ancient, beautiful, and complicated game — the charm of which is indeed largely due to its complication — has much fascination. It was played in France in some form or other so far back as the thirteenth century. In the following century it was introduced into many French towns, and buildings were adapted, or constructed, for the purposes of the game. These were called tripots, and we hear of the erection early in the fifteenth century of a tripot in Paris in the Rue Grenier Saint Lazare, called Le Petit Temple, in which one Margot, a woman, used to play in about 1427, with such skill that she could hold her own with all but the best players of the opposite sex. The game in which she was so proficient is spoken of as "hand-ball," and there is other evidence to show that, up to the beginning of the sixteenth century, the hand had not been entirely superseded by the racket, as the weapon with which the ball was struck.

Of the professional tennis-players, who, in modern times, have attained the highest distinction in the tennis-courts at home and abroad, the name of J. Edmond Barre, the great French player, stands pre-eminent. Mr. J.M. Heathcote, an accomplished writer on tennis, and perhaps the greatest of all amateur players of the game, has placed on record his opinion of Barre as being "the finest all-round player the world ever produced or is likely to produce". Barre, who died in 1873, appears, indeed, to have been much superior to any of his contemporaries, and to have enjoyed a special reputation as a match-player of extraordinary staying power, and a remarkable giver of odds. Another great French player is Charles Delahaye, nicknamed "Biboche", who, in his prime, was inferior only to Barre. He has long since been on the retired list; and the leading professional players in Paris, at the present time, are Ferdinand, and G. Lesueur, known as "Le Biscon".

Hit out on the line of flight
A return on the same line as the shot received.

Hitting deep
Hitting to an area on or within 2 or 3 feet of the base line.

Hitting short
Hitting into an area in the vicinity of the service line.

Hoad, Lewis Alan
Australia (born 1934) — He won Wimbledon men's singles in 1956,

1957, French 1956, Australian 1956. In four Davis Cup Challenge Rounds won eight rubbers of the 11 he contested.

Hold service

The winning of a game by the player serving. Opposite of 'service break'.

Hop

The bound of the ball.

Hotchkiss, Hazel

USA (1886-1974) — Won USA women's singles in 1909, 1910, 1911 and 1919. Never beaten when paired with Helen Wills Moody, they won Wimbledon doubles in 1924 and the USA doubles six times between 1909 and 1928.

How?

The call of a player for the decision of the linesman or umpire on any doubtful ball.

I

I.O.C.
International Olympics Committee.

I.T.F.
International Tennis Federation. The world rulers of the game comprising about 100 affiliated national tennis associations. It was founded in 1913, the founder members being Australasia (comprising Australia and New Zealand), Austria, Belgium, Denmark, France, Germany, Great Britain, Netherlands, Russia, South Africa, Spain, Sweden and Switzerland. It comprises full members with weighted voting rights varying according to the strength of lawn tennis in the nation concerned and associate members without voting rights. The maximum voting strength, 12, belongs to Australia, France, Great Britain and the United States.

I.T.F. World Champions
A panel of former champions decide annually who are the International Tennis Federation's World Champions.

Men

1978 Bjorn Borg (Swe)
1979 Bjorn Borg (Swe)
1980 Bjorn Borg (Swe)
1981 John McEnroe (USA)
1982 Jimmy Connors (USA)
1983 John McEnroe (USA)
1984 John McEnroe (USA)
1985 Ivan Lendl (Cz)

1986 Ivan Lendl (Cz)
1987 Ivan Lendl (Cz)
1988 Mats Wilander (Swe)
1989 Boris Becker (FRG)

Women

1978 Chris Evert (USA)
1979 Martina Navratilova (Cs)
1980 Chris Evert Lloyd (USA)
1981 Chris Evert Lloyd (USA)
1982 Martina Navratilova (USA)
1983 Martina Navratilova (USA)
1984 Martina Navratilova (USA)
1985 Martina Navratilova (USA)
1986 Martina Navratilova (USA)
1987 Steffi Graf (W. Ger)
1988 Steffi Graf (W. Ger)
1989 Steffi Graf (W. Ger)

In

A ball that bounces within the applicable boundaries of the court.

India

Tennis was brought in India by the British in 1880 and regular championships were started at the Lahore Gymkhana in 1885—the Punjab Championships. Others followed but slowly, and not until 1920 did the popularity of tennis and the number of its clubs and players necessitate the formation of a national association, the All India Lawn Tennis Association.

The first All-India championships was held in 1910, with men's and women's events. India made an auspicious Davis Cup debut in 1921 by beating France 4-1 and reaching the semi-finals, where Japan proved too strong. India has dominated the Cup's Eastern Zone since its introduction in 1955. In 1966 India beat Brazil, conquerors of the USA, to reach the Challenge Round where a strong Australian team won 4-1. 1974 provided a sad upset, with India reaching the final and seemingly, becoming favourites to beat South Africa and capture the Cup. Political factors intervened, the Government prohibiting the team from playing the South Africans because they practised racial/colour apartheid. Again in 1987 India made the finals beating Australia 3-2 in the semis. In the final India lost 1-4 to Sweden. India staged the first and subsequent Asian Championship and has administered the Davis Cup Special Travelling Expenses Fun (Eastern Zone) for many years.

Top class players have developed over the years, with Ramanathan Krishnan, Ramesh Krishnan, Vijay Amritraj, Anand Amritraj, Leander Paes, Ramanathan Krishnan was their best, twice a Wimbledon singles semi-finalist, he won the junior event there in 1954, an achievement repeated by his son Ramesh Krishnan in 1979.

In Wimbledon Ramanathan Krishnan reached the semi-finals in 1960 and then again in 1961. Jan Kodes defeated Vijay Amritraj in 1973 Wimbledon semi-finals.

Injuries

Tennis is a healthy sport; nevertheless injuries can occur. To know the danger is to lessen the risks. However, in a contact game of the nature of tennis, accidents and injuries can happen and the medical advice in this section could prove of considerable importance in reducing the effect of injury and enabling a player to get back into the game more quickly. It is useful for every player, as well as referee or linesman or coach, to recognize the symptoms of the more serious injuries. As would be expected with such a hard-hitting contact sport, most of the typical tennis injuries are due to direct or indirect impact rather than over-use. Cuts, grazes, bruises, sprains, strains, dislocation and fractures are commonplace. Every part of the body has a blacklist of likely injuries.

1. Skin and subcutaneous tissue
2. Feet

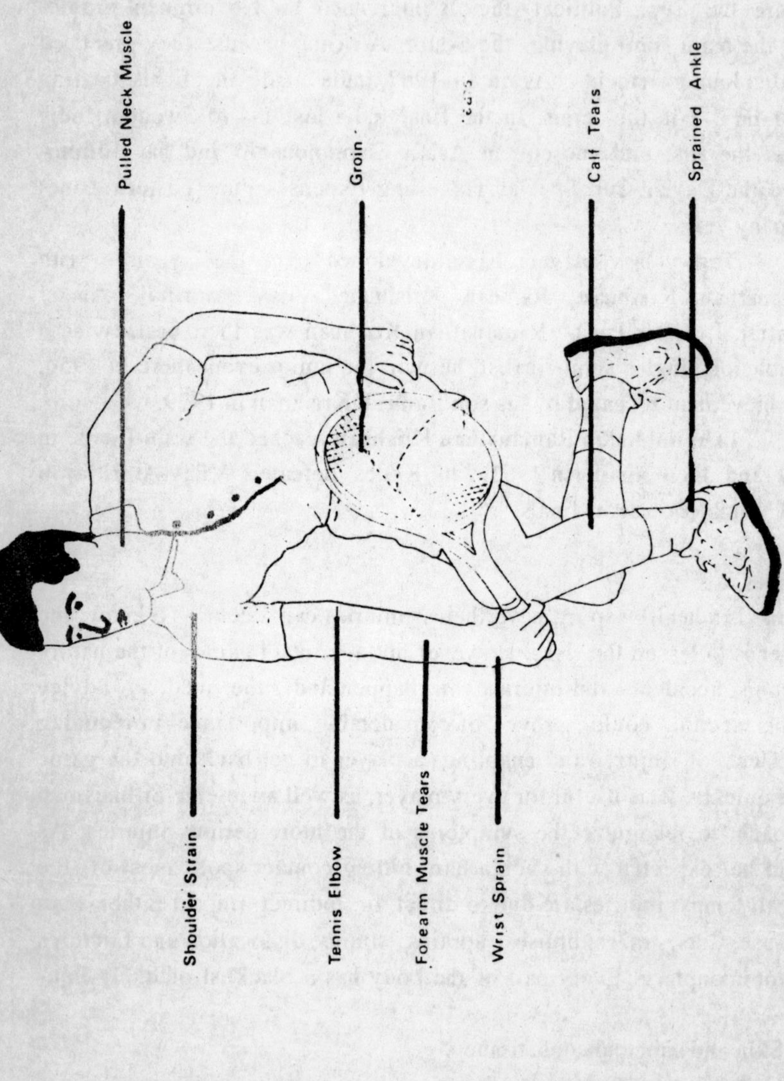
Pulled Neck Muscle
Groin
Calf Tears
Sprained Ankle
Shoulder Strain
Tennis Elbow
Forearm Muscle Tears
Wrist Sprain

3. Pulled and torn muscles
4. Calf tears
5. Forearm tears
6. Abdominal strain
7. Thigh tears
8. Tendons
9. Tennis shoulder
10. Tennis elbow
11. Wrist strain
12. Groin strain
13. Sprained knee
14. Eye injuries
15. Backbone
16. Foot complaints
17. Toes

In play

A ball is in play from the moment at which it is delivered in service until the point has been decided.

Invitation tournament

A tournament, usually staged without securing official sanction from the relevant association. It is open to invited players only.

Italian Championships

An Italian Championship was first staged in 1894 and the men's singles winner was G. de Martino. The game was played in Italy as early as 1878 when an English Club was founded in Bordighera. An Italian Lawn Tennis Association was founded in Rome in 1894 but lasted only four years. It was re-formed in Florence in 1910. The Italian International Championship first held in 1930.

J

Jacobs, Helen Hull

USA (born 1908) — Won Wimbledon women's singles in 1936 and the USA singles in 1932-35, losing to Alice Marble in the 1936 final, a run of successes precisely paralleled by Chris Evert-Lloyd in 1975-78 and her loss in the 1979 final.

Jausovec, Mima

Yugoslavia (born 1956) — She won the Italian Open in 1976, the French the following year and the German Open a year later. Her highest ranking was 9th in 1977 and, paired with Virginia Ruzici, she won the German, French and Italian doubles titles in 1978.

Jedrzejowska, Jadwiga

Poland (born 1911) — Poland's outstanding woman player. Her major international success was as finalist to Dorothy Round at Wimbledon and to Anita Lizana in the US singles in 1937. She headed Poland's ranking list first in 1928. She headed every subsequent ranking list up to and including that of 1959, a supremacy lasting 30 years.

Johnston, William M.

USA (1894-1946) — 'Little Bill', a Californian, small in physique but a brilliant volleyer and the possessor of a formidable top-spin forehand, was 'Big Bill' Tiden's principal rival at home in the first half of the 1920s. He beat Hunter in the 1923 Wimbledon final, losing only one set in the tournament. He won the US doubles with Griffin 1915/16 and 1920 and played in eight Davis Cup challenge rounds, winning 18 of his 21 Davis Cup rubbers.

Jones, Mrs. P.F.

UK (born 1938) — The top British player every year from 1962 to 1967 who combined intelligence with doggedness on the court. Her left-handed strokes were rarely spectacular but she wielded an all round game with shrewdness above the normal. She was a quarter-finalist in the Wimbledon singles 9 times between 1958 and 1968 and finalist in 1967. She was also US finalist in 1961 and 1967. Before taking up lawn tennis seriously she was a noted table tennis player and five times a finalist for a world championship.

Junior and Senior Grand Slam Champions

Only three junior Wimbledon champs went on to become men's champion. They are: Bjorn Borg, Pat Cash and Stefan Edberg. Anne Haydon Jones and Karen Hantze Susman are the only women to have repeated their junior triumph in the seniors. Mats Wilander and Ivan Lendl have won both the junior and senior titles at the French Open; Hana Mandlikova is the only woman to have done so. A total of 12 Australian junior boy champions went on to claim the men's title. In chronological order they are: Jack Crawford, Viv McGrath, Adrian Quist, John Bromwich, Dinny Pails, Frank Sedgman, Ken McGregor, Ken Rosewall, Lew Hoad, Rod Laver, John Newcombe and Stefan Edberg. Four junior girl champions have also claimed the women's trophy: Joan Hartigan, Kerry Melville Reid, Evonne Goolagong, and Christine O'Neil. No US junior singles winner has won the senior title.

K

Kill

An overhead, powerful volley (smash) placed beyond the opponent's reach or hit so forcefully that he cannot return the ball.

King, Billie Jean

USA (born 1943) — Mrs. King is the only woman to win US singles titles on all four surfaces — grass, indoor, clay and hard courts. Her achievements were interspersed with three knee operations and ankle surgery. Beat Elizabeth Ryan's record of 19 Wimbledon Championship titles on 7 July, 1979, one day after the death of Miss Ryan who had said she never wanted to see her record beaten. The most outstanding woman in the history of tennis since Suzanne Lenglen. Founder and first president of the Women's Tennis Association, she and her husband Larry pioneered World Team Tennis, the ill-fated project for inter-city league play. Her unremitting drive raised women tennis players from second class appendages to men into a multi-million profession. Won Wimbledon singles six times, French singles once, Australian once and USA four times.

King's Cup

The King of Sweden's Cup, an international men's indoor team championships, was originally played on a challenge round basis and then, from 1952, as a straight knock-out competition. The European Tennis Association took control in 1975 and the competition has been on a league basis, with home and away ties, each comprising two singles and a doubles, since 1976.

Knock-up

Practice play generally to warm up before a match, and often played without serving or scoring; sometimes only knocking the balls back and forth over the net regardless of the court lines.

Kodes, Jan

Czechoslovakia (born 1946) — A dogged, industrious player with great strength and determination. He won his first major victories on clay, winning the French singles 1970/71 and reaching the Italian final 1970/71/72, but he won the Wimbledon singles in the boycott year of 1973 and was runner-up in the US Championships in 1971/73. He first represented Czechoslovakia in Davis Cup in 1966, took them to the final in 1975 and was a member of their winning team in 1980.

Kramer, Jack Albert

USA (born 1921) — A methodical and powerful exponent of the serve and volley game. Won Wimbledon singles title in 1947 after losing dramatically to the then unknown Jaroslay Drobney in 1946. Won doubles 1946/47. Won US singles 1946/47 and doubles 1940/41/43/47 and doubles 1940/41/43/47.

Krishnan, Ramanathan

India (born 1937) — India's most powerful and fluent player. A Wimbledon semi-finalist in 1960 and 1961. Played Davis Cup for India 1953 to 1968. Best world ranking No. 6 in 1961.

Krishnan, Ramesh

India (born 1961) — His game contains an impressive array of shots and he has pulled off a list of big wins already, including victories over Stan Smith and Gene Mayer. He beat them on his way to the quarters of the US Open in 1981. He followed in the footsteps of his father, Ramanathan, by playing Davis Cup for India. The highlights of his amateur career were the junior title wins at both the French and Wimbledon championship in 1979.

L

L.T.A.

The Lawn Tennis Association, the game's ruling body in England, Scotland and Wales. It was founded in 1888. It is administered by a council consisting of representatives from the English county associations, from the national association of Scotland and Wales and from some other representative lawn tennis bodies including the All England Lawn Tennis Club where the Wimbledon Championships are staged.

L.T.F.

Lawn Tennis Foundation, an organization sponsored mainly by manufacturers for promoting tennis in Britain.

Lacoste, Rene

France (born 1905) — In tennis the French Revolution didn't happen until 1924. It was worth the wait. Four Gallic stars, the "four musketeers," shone at the same time. Jean Borotra, "the Bounding Basque," was an extremely elegant stylist who led with his backhand and coveted a position close to the net.

The sloe-eyed Frenchman who his native Nationals in 1925, 1927 and 1929. He toppled Jean Borotra in 1926 in the only all-French final of the US Championships and captured Wimbledon in 1925 and 1928.

Latitudinally

From side to side.

Laver, Rodney George

Australia (born 1938) — Laver has won two French, two US titles and four Wimbledons, a modern record. But his most amazing feat was his triumph in the 1971 Tennis Champions Classic. He appeared in four successive Wimbledon finals, losing to Alex Olmedo in 1959. His last notable achievement was joining Newcombe, at the age of 35, to beat the US in the 1973 Davis Cup final at Cleveland.

Laver, Rodney George

Australia (born 1938) — The first player to achieve the Grand Slam twice and the master of the old professional circuit, with Rosewall as his great rival, in its last days. A left-hander, red-haired like Budge, with a spectacularly aggressive style, he brought off the slam of the four major singles titles, as an amateur, in 1962 and then, as a professional, in 1969. A member of the undefeated Australian Davis Cup team from 1959-62. He returned to Davis Cup in 1973, collecting three more rubbers in Australia's 5-0 victory over the US in the final at Cleveland.

Left court (player)

The partner of a doubles team who receives service in the left court. The left court is also referred to as the odd court or the backhand court, since usually the player with the stronger backhand plays the left court.

Lendl, Ivan

Czechoslovakia (born 1960) — Lendl is 6 ft. 2 in tall — a thrilling and powerful player when he is able to win on his own terms. Yet he seems to lack the flexibility of shot to cope with an opponent who is able to absorb his aggression and dent the confidence which is vital to his game. Ranked No. 1 from 1985 to 1988, Ivan Lendl is the greatest Czech tennis star of all time and one of the hardest-ever hitters of the ball. He was an outstanding junior player, winning titles at Wimbledon, Paris and Rome in 1978. He quickly made his mark in the senior game, and was in the top ten by 1980. He won seven Grand Prix titles that year, and reached the final of the Masters in New York in January 1981, losing to Bjorn Borg in four sets.

At Wimbledon Lendl has yet to reproduce the devastating form that other audiences have come to expect from him.

Lenglen, Suzanne

France (1899-1938) — She established her fame by winning the first post-World War I Wimbledon championship in 1919, beating Mrs. Lambert Chambers in a memorable Challenge Round after being match points down. Until 1926, her only defeat in singles was in the American championships of 1921 when she was ill and retired to Mrs. Molla Mallory after losing the first set 2-6. She was a fine volleyer, strong overhead and electric in her mobility. Her accuracy of stroke was prodigious. Wimbledon champion (singles) 1919, 1920, 1921, 1922, 1923, 1925; (doubles) 1919, 1920, 1921, 1922, 1923, 1925; (mixed) 1920, 1922, 1925.

Length

The distance a ball travels after crossing the net; specifically, how close it strikes to the base line.

Let

A term common to many ball games to describe the replaying of a point without penalty in the event of an unusual occurrence. In tennis, a let is played if the service hits the net and bounces into the service court or touches the receiver and anything he carries.

Let ball

Any point which is played over because of some kind of interference.

Let it touch!

The warning called out by a player to his partner in doubles, when he thinks a ball is going out.

Let service

A serve which touches the net tape and falls into the proper square and is played over.

Lift stroke

A stroke made with the racket nearly or quite vertical, and drawn up sharply as it meets the ball, apparently lifting the ball over the net.

Lindqvist, Catarina

Sweden (born 1983) — She has for years been the standard bearer for Swedish women's tennis. It is both the joy and the pain of her life. On the one hand she enjoys the recognition accorded to her as a trailblazer. Her achievements — such as being the first Swedish woman to get as far as the semi-finals at Wimbledon in 1989.

Line ball

A ball that strikes any portion of the line (outside edge, middle, or inside edge). Such a ball is considered to be good.

Line of flight

The direction of the shot.

Line pass

A stroke made from the side of the court so as to drive the ball past the player at the net, the ball passing parallel with and inside the side line.

Lines

The various markings (or lines) which identify the playing areas and boundaries of a court.

Linesman

An official of the match, whose duty it is to call faults and to decide whether balls are inside or outside base, service, and side lines.

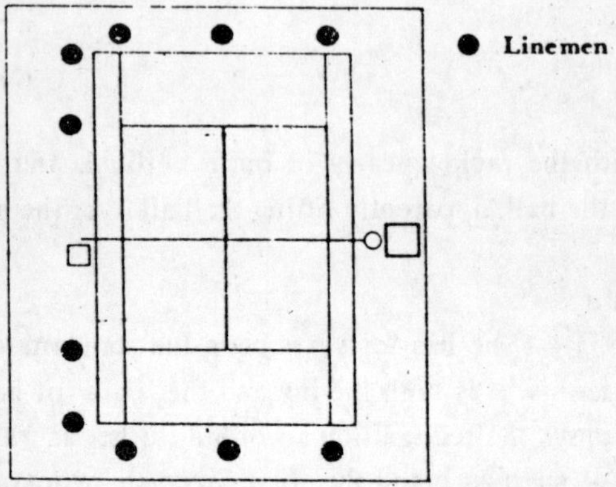

Live hand

A firm but not viselike grip; not frozen or tightened up. Same as life-in-the-hand.

Lloyd, Chris

USA (born 1954) — Chris is unbeaten in Wightman Cup singles (22 victories) and also in the Federation Cup (28). Her 56 match-winning streak in 1974 is a women's record and she also holds the record for most consecutive victories on one surface: 125 on clay from August 1973 to May 1979. Wimbledon saw the end of an astonishing record in 1983 when Chris Lloyd was beaten in the third round by a fellow American, Kathy Jordan. It was the first time Mrs. Lloyd had been defeated before the semi-final round in the 34 Grand Slam tournaments in which she had played since 1971.

Lob

A ball hit so that its flight goes high into the air (usually over the reach of the net player) and deep in the opponent's backcourt. A lob volley has a similar trajectory but is hit before the ball has bounced and is considered to be a very advanced and very delicate shot.

A
1
2
3

Lob volley
A shot hit high into the air from a volleying position.

Long
A ball bouncing outside the baseline.

Longest matches
At Warsaw in 1966 England's Roger Taylor defeated Wieslaw Gasiorek of Poland 27-29, 31-29, 6-4 (a total of 126 games) in a King's Cup match at Warsaw. Ironically, the longest women's match took place the same year. American Kathy Blake defeated Mexican Elena Subirats 12-10, 6-8, 14-12 in a New York tournament.

Longest men's match
In a 1982 Davis Cup quarter-final tie at St. Louis, John EcEnroe took six hours 22 minutes and five sets to defeat 17-year-old Mats Wilander on a "fast" supreme court.

Longest tiebreak
The Swedish-Danish combination of Jan Gunnarsson and Michael Mortensen defeated Australia's John Frawley and Paraguay's Victor Pecci in a fourth set tiebreak which went at 26-24, at Wimbledon, 1985.

Longest women's match
A first round match between Vicki Nelson and Jean Hepner at the Ginny of Richmond event in September 1984 is the longest match in terms of time duration in tennis history. Nelson won 6-4, 7-6 (13-11) after six hours 31 minutes. The tiebreak alone took an hour 47 minutes. One point in the tiebreak lasted 29 minutes, during which the ball whizzed over the net 643 times!

Longitudinally
From back to front.

Loop drive

A groundstroke that is hit softer than the conventional drive. The ball travels in an arc rather than on a direct line.

Love

Term used in scoring to mean zero or nothing. This word probably came from the French word "I'oueff" which means goose egg, and when the game was taken to England, the French word was pronounced like "love". A love game is won without the loss of a point, and if you win a love set you have won six games, and your opponent has won none. When you are told that a player has won a match "love and love," this means the opponent did not win a game.

Love game (set)

A game completed without the loser winning a point: or set won without conceding a game.

Love game

A game in which one side has not scored a point.

Love-one, (love-two, love-three, love-four or love-five)

A term used in scoring sets to indicate that the server has not won a game.

Love-set

A set in which one side did not win a single game. In England, winning six successive games is called a love set, even though the antagonist had already scored when the run began.

Lutz, Bob

USA (born 1947) — One of the all-time great doubles players, Lutz and Stan Smith won four US Opens and were three times runners-up at Wimbledon. He and Smith are also the only pair to have won the US national titles on all four surfaces: grass, clay, hard court and indoor.

Luxembourg

Lawn tennis has been played in Luxembourg since the end of the 19th century. The Luxembourg Lawn Tennis Association was founded in 1946 and affiliated to the I.L.T.F. the same year.

M

Major championship

Four international championships are rated 'major' by the I.L.T.F.— the Australian, French, All England (Wimbledon), and United States. The tennis grand slam constitutes winning all four in the same year.

Mandlikova, Hana

Czechoslovakia (born 1962) — A beautiful, elegant mover on court, as befits a girl whose father competed for Czechoslovakia in 1956 and 1960 Olympic Games as a sprinter. 'Hana' learned her tennis watching Martina Navratilova at the Sparta Club in Prague. She fulfilled her potential by capturing the French title in 1981 and then reached the Wimbledon final where she froze against Chris Lloyd. A rather disappointing 1982 was highlighted by an appearance in the US Open final — where she again lost easily to Mrs. Lloyd.

Marble, Alice

USA (born 1913) — One of the most striking of aggressive American women players who brought the serve-volley technique to unheard of heights and held by many to be the most effective player of all times. Wimbledon champion (singles) 1939; (doubles) 1938, 1939; mixed 1937, 1938, 1939.

Marker

The instrument to mark out the lines of a court.

Masters

The play-off climax to the Grand Prix.

Match

A predetermined number of sets, usually two out of three or three out of five sets, which decide the winner.

Match point

When a player requires one point to win the match, he is said to hold match point; if say, he leads 40-15, he has two match points. Likewise, the terms 'set point', game point and a point for a break (of service) are also used.

Mathieu, Simone

France (1908-1980) — A formidable clay court player, she succeeded Lenglen as the leader of the women's game in France. She was junior champion — as a married woman — at 18, and 3 years later reached the French final. She won the French doubles 6 times and the Wimbledon doubles twice with Ryan 1933/34 and once with Yorke 1937.

Maureen Connolly Cup

USA versus Great Britain, women under 21, maximum of 5 players each side. First held in 1973.

Mayer, Alex Sandy

USA (born 1952) — The older of the two Mayer brothers, Sandy is fierce critic of the on-court behaviour of many of his colleagues and wants to see the sport cleaned up. He made his first big impression on the tennis world in 1973 when he became the N.C.A.A. singles and doubles champion and grabbed all the headliners at Wimbledon the same year by upsetting the favourite Ilie Nastase. Together, the brothers won the 1979 French Open doubles as well as the US Pro Championship in 1980.

Mayer, Gene

USA (born 1956) — He hits the ball two-handed on both sides with a rare command of touch and angle. His older brother, Sandy, with whom he won the 1979 French doubles title, says that Gene has so many different types of game 'if one isn't working he throws it away and tries another'. Apart from his achievements on court, Gene's voracious appetite for food is legendary.

McEnroe, John

USA (born 1959) — McEnroe is the most brilliant and most temperamental player. At his best, he has elevated tennis to an art form with near perfect displays of stroke skill and tactics. But his whole career has been marred by outbursts of arrogance, rudeness and sullenness which have severely harmed the professional image of the game and reduced its disciplinary powers to farce. At Wimbledon in 1983 when he recaptured the men's title with a performance in the final which was almost angelic in its benevolence. After devastating the unseeded Chris Lewis 6-2, 6-2, 6-2 in an incident-free contest which was the quickest men's final of the Open era, he kissed the Challenge Cup and shook hands with every official within reach.

His career as a professional has been sprinkled with brilliant matches, including the unforgettable 1980 Wimbledon final against Borg which the Swede won 1-6, 7-5, 6-3, 6-7 and 8-6 after McEnroe had captured the fourth set on a tie-break of 34 points. McEnroe went on to prove his class by beating Borg in the US final in the same year and repeating the process at Wimbledon, and Flushing Meadow in 1981— the latter victory making him the first American to win the US title three successive times since Bill Tilden in the 1920s.

McGregor, Ken

Australia (born 1929) — He won Australian men's singles in 1952. In 1951 he won the Grand Slam of men's doubles championships. He was also a good Australian-rules footballer.

McKane, Kathleen

UK (born 1897) — Twice winner of the Wimbledon singles in 1924 and 1926.

McLoughlin, Maurice

USA (1890-1957) — In his debut at Wimbledon 1913 his personality, sportsmanship and fiery service took him into the Challenge Round against Tony Wilding. Won the USA singles in 1912, 1913 and doubles in 1912, 1913 and 1914.

Men's Grand Prix masters

Throughout the season various tournaments count towards the Masters and points are gained according to performances.

Singles

1970	Stan Smith	USA
1971	Ilie Nastase	Rom
1972	Ilie Nastase	Rom
1973	Ilie Nastase	Rom
1974	Guillermo Vilas	Arg
1975	Ilie Nastase	Rom
1976	Manuel Orantes	Spa
1978	Jimmy Connors	USA
1979	John McEnroe	USA
1980	Bjorn Borg	Swe
1981	Bjorn Borg	Swe
1982	Ivan Lendl	Cz
1983	Ivan Lendl	Cz
1984	John McEnroe	USA
1985	John McEnroe	USA
1986	Ivan Lendl	Cz
1987	Ivan Lendl	Cz
1988	Boris Becker	W.Ger
1989	Stefan Edberg	Swe

Doubles

1970	Arthur Ashe, Stan Smith (USA)
1971	Not held
1972	Not held

1973 Not held
1974 Not held
1975 Juan Gisbert, Manuel Orantes (Spa)
1976 Fred McNair, Sherwood Stewart (USA)
1978 Bob Hewitt, Frew McMillan (S.Af)
1979 Peter Fleming, John McEnroe (USA)
1980 Peter Fleming, John McEnroe (USA)
1981 Peter Fleming, John McEnroe (USA)
1982 Peter Fleming, John McEnroe (USA)
1983 Peter Fleming, John McEnroe (USA)
1984 Peter Fleming, John McEnroe (USA)
1985 Peter Fleming, John McEnroe (USA)
1986 Stefan Edberg, Anders Jarryd (Swe)
1987 Miloslav Mecir, Tomas Smid (Cz)
1988 Rick Leach, Jim Pugh (USA)
1989 Patrick McEnroe, Jim Grabb (USA)

Mid-court

The area in front or in back of the service line of the playing court.

M.I.P.T.C.

Men's International Professional Tennis Council. The ruling body of the men's professional game, comprising representatives of the I.T.F., A.T.P. and tournaments.

Miss

Failure to hit the ball with the racket.

Mixed doubles

A match between two pairs, each of which consists of a male and female.

Mix-up

Changing the pace of play; varying your shots.

Modifying the stroke
Adapting the stroke to incorrect body position in relation to the ball.

Moody, Helen Wills
USA (born 1905) — She won Wimbledon's singles 8 times in 9 challenges. She was beaten in the final by Kitty McKane in 1924, won in 1927 and then for the last time in 1938. 'Little Poker Face', as she was known, was emotionless and deadly on the court, possessed accurate and persistent driving power.

N

Nastase, Ilie

Romania (1946) — Won French singles in 1973 and Grand Prix Masters singles in 1971, 1972, 1973 and 1975.

Nations Cup

The men's international team championship organised by the Association of Tennis Professionals. The format of each tie comprises two singles and a doubles. The competition is restricted to eight teams, the eligibility of the first seven being governed by the relative standing of the nation's two best players on the A.T.P. ranking list.

Navratilova, Martina

USA (born 1956) — The highest-earning tennis player of all time. She was eleven when the Russian tanks rolled into Prague, and her world changed for ever. Born into a family dedicated to sport, she had played tennis since the age of four and was already dreaming of the Centre Court at Wimbledon. Soon her tennis was to take her abroad — West Germany, France and finally that 'magic place', America — and though she loved Czechoslovakia she began bitterly to resent the restrictions that were imposed on her.

She was eighteen when she left for America, but she soon found new pressures took the place of those she left behind. Her vivid personality seemed to attract the spotlight of publicity.

Her catalogue of major titles runs as follows:

***French** (singles winner)* 1982, 1984,

(doubles winner) 1975, 1982, 1984, 1985, 1986, 1987, 1988

(mixed winner) 1974, 1985

Wimbledon* *(singles winner) 1978, 1979, 1982, 1983, 1984, 1985, 1986, 1987, 1990

(doubles winner) 1976, 1979, 1981, 1982, 1983, 1984, 1986

(mixed winner) 1985

US Open* *(singles winner) 1983, 1984, 1986, 1987

(doubles winner) 1977, 1978, 1980, 1983, 1984, 1986, 1987, 1989

(mixed winner) 1985, 1987

Australian* *(singles winner) 1981, 1983, 1985

(doubles winner) 1980, 1982, 1983, 1984, 1985, 1987, 1988, 1989

Women's World Series : 1979, 1982, 1983, 1984, 1985, 1986.

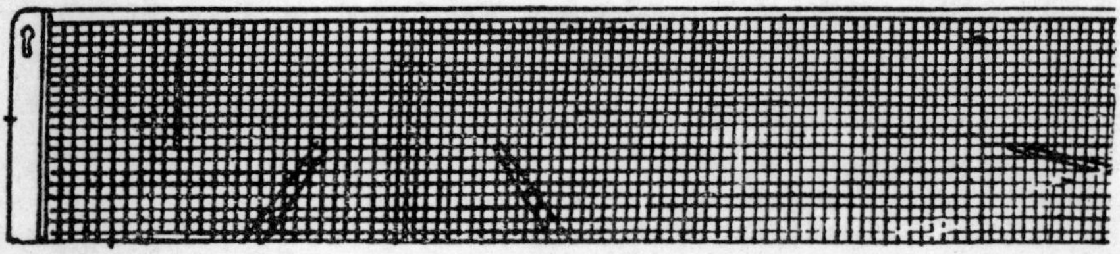

Net

The netting placed across the middle of the court. It is suspended by a cord or metal cable the ends of which are attached to two posts.

Net ball

A ball that touches the net while travelling from end to end of the court. Except for a service, which is called a 'let', such a ball remains in play.

Net cord

When a player hits the ball and it hits the top of the net (the cord) and goes over the net (often dropping dead in an unplayable position), the player making the shot is often, justly, described as having had a 'lucky net cord'.

Net game

A strategy in which a player attempts to play mostly in the forecourt, close to the net, where he can win his points with volleys and overheads.

Net man

In doubles play, this is the partner who stays close to the net while the other remains near the baseline. Generally used in connection with the server.

Net play

Action occurring near to the net.

Net stick

Used to support the net during singles play at 42 inches when placed on singles side line. Same as singles stick or side stick.

New balls

During play, the covering of balls becomes scuffed; so that the balls used are consistent in behaviour. Balls are replaced at regular intervals in important matches.

Newcombe, John David

Australia (born 1944) — The supreme exponent of the simple, rugged style in modern tennis. Splendidly confident and with great strength of personality, Newcombe relied upon a heavy service, forceful volleying and solid, powerful groundstrokes. His best singles successes were on grass — Wimbledon 1967, 1970/71, US Championships 1967, 1973, and Australia 1973, 1975. He first played in the Davis Cup in 1963 and finally against Italy in Rome, 1976, but perhaps his best performance was in 1973 when he and Laver inflicted a 5-0 defeat upon the United States at Cleveland.

Noah, Yannick

France (born 1960) — The son of a First Division footballer in the French Cameroons, West Africa, Noah was discovered by America's great black champion Arthur Ashe during a tennis clinic in 1971. Ashe immediately contacted the French authorities and Noah was enlisted into their tennis school in Nice. His first major tour success came in 1981 — in Ashe's hometown of Richmond, Virginia. Noah, performing like a man possessed, crushed Gene Mayer, Roscoe Tanner and Ivan Lendl (who withdrew at 6-1, 3-1) to take the title.

No man's land

A general area within the baseline and proper net position area where, when the player is caught, he must volley or hit ground strokes near his feet.

Non-Porous Court (Impervious)

Is one on which water does not penetrate, but runs off the surface.

Norton, Brian I.C.

S. Africa (1899-1957) — A highly talented, all round player who was involved in dramatic happenings at Wimbledon in 1920. He survived match points to win the All Comers' final against Spaniard Manuel Alonso but then, having had two match balls, lost in the Challenge Round to his friend Tilden.

Not up

Refers to a double bounce. This term is used by an umpire when a player fails to play the ball before the second bounce.

Nuthall, Betty

UK (born 1911) — Now Mrs. Shoemaker. An aggressive and attractive competitor, with a remarkable record as a junior, she never progressed beyond quarter-final at Wimbledon but gained her most impressive victories abroad. She played in 8 World Cup matches between 1927 and 1939, winning 6 rubbers and losing 7.

O

Objective hit

A planned shot carefully directed to a point in the opposite court to do the striker most good and the opponent least good.

Odd court

The left court since, whenever play is started in this court, an odd number of points has been played in the current game.

Offensive lob

A ball hit just above the racket reach of an opposing net player.

Offensive volley

A volleying stroke made from above net level. Also called high volley.

Officials

A lot of tennis matches which are played in the parks, at school, or

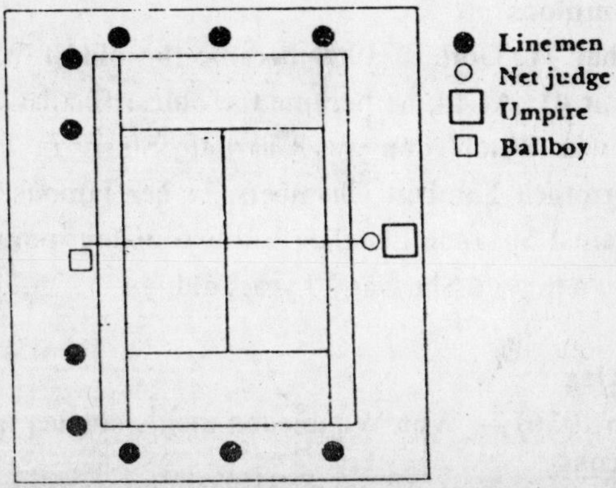

at club level do not have any umpires or officials in charge of the game, in which case the players make their own decisions and class. Sometimes an argument ensues over whether a ball is 'in' or 'out', and in friendly matches this is often resolved by replaying the point. In general, players call their own lines on their side of the net. In more serious competitions, the L.T.A. Code of Conduct is used.

In tournaments, even those at junior level, it is quite common for an umpire to be in charge of a match. In top-class events on the professional tennis circuit, for example The All England Championships at Wimbledon, there are several officials in charge of a match.

First, there is the refree, who takes overall charge of a tournament and is often called onto the court when an appeal is made against the umpire. The referee's decision on a question of law then becomes final. The referee has the power to postpone a match at any time because of failing light, bad ground conditions or bad weather. The match score remains the same during any postponement of play and, if possible, the match should resume on the same court. The umpire calls the score (and records it on the score sheet). He also decides disputed points.

Other officials at the tennis tournament would be the assistants to the umpire: the linesmen, the net-cord judges, and the foot-fault judges, who help the umpire by calling the ball out, calling a fault, let, etc.

Oldest champions

Briton Arthur W. Gore in 1909 became the oldest Wimbledon singles champion at 41. At 44, he became the oldest finalist ever. The oldest woman to win Wimbledon was Charlotte Sterry in 1908, age 37, although Dorrothea Lambert Chambers, in her famous challenge round defence against Suzanne Lenglen, had two match points to become the oldest woman to win. She was 40 years old.

Olmedo, Alex

Peru (born 1936) — Won Wimbledon men's singles in 1959 and USA singles in 1958.

Olympic Games

Lawn Tennis was included in the Olympic Games from 1896 to 1924 and as a demonstration sport in 1988.

Men's Singles

1896	John Boland (UK)
1900	Hugh Doherty (UK)
1904	Beals Wright (USA)
1906	Max Decugis (Fra)
1908	Josiah Ritchie (UK)
	Arthur Gore (UK)
1912	Charles Winslow (S Af)
	Andre Gobert (Fra)
1920	Louis Raymond (SAf)
1924	Vince Richards (USA)
1988	Miloslav Mecir (Cz)

Men's Doubles

1896	John Boland (Ire), Fritz Traun (Ger)
1900	Reginald, Hugh Doherty (UK)
1904	Beals Wright, Edger Leonard (USA)
1906	Max Decugis, Maurice Germot (Fra)
1908	George Hillyard, Reginald Doherty (UK)
	Arthur Gore, Herbert Roper Harrett (UK)
1912	Charles Winslow, Harold Kitson (SAf)
	Andre Gobert,Maurice Germot (Fra)
1920	Oswal Turnbull, Max Woosnam (UK)
1924	Vince Richards, Frank Hunter (UK)
1988	Ken Flach, Robert Seguso (USA)

Women's Singles

1900	Charlotte Cooper (UK)
1906	Esmee Simiriotou (Ger)
1908	Dorothea Lambert Chambers (UK)
	Gwendoline Eastlake-Smith (UK)

1912 Marguerite Broqudis (Fra)
Edith Hannam (UK)
1920 Suzanne Lenglen (Fra)
1924 Helen Wills (USA)
1988 Steffi Graf (W.Ger)

Women's Doubles
1920 Winifred McNair, Kathleen McKane (UK)
1924 Hazel Wightman, Helen Wills (USA)
1988 Pam Shriver, Zina Garrison (USA)

Mixed Doubles
1900 Reginald Doherty, Charlotte Cooper (UK)
1906 Max and Marie Decugis (Fra)
1912 Heinrich Schomburgk, Dora Konig (Ger)
Percy Dixon, Edith Hannam (UK)
1920 Max Decugis, Suzanne Lenglen (Fra)
1924 Norris Williams, Hazel Wightman (USA)

On the rise

The term used to describe an aggressive style of play in which a player returns the ball before it reaches the height of its bounces. By playing the ball early or on the rise, you give your opponent less time to get set for your return. This style of play is usually not advocated for beginners.

One-love, two-love, three-love, etc.

A term used in scoring to indicate that the server has one (two, three, etc.) games and the opponent none.

Open face racket

A racket whose face is moving under the ball. A wide open racket face is parallel to the court surface.

Open tennis

All games, matches, competitions, etc. which are open to all categories of players. This virtually universal abandonment of varying categories and their replacement by the one word 'players' came into force in 1968.

Open tournament

Any tournament that accepts entries from all categories of players, including those under contract to outside agents and not subject to control by national associations.

Opening

A defensive lapse or mistake which permits a player an opportunity to score a point.

Orantes, Manuel

Spain (born 1949) — A consummate artist on European clay whose exquisite touch and gentle, generous manners made him an international favourite. A left-hander who, after leading Spain to two Galea Cup victories in 1968 and 1969, won his first two important titles in 1972.

Out

Term used when a ball bounces outside the playing area.

Out of position shot

A stroke made when the player or his posture is in a disadvantageous position.

Overdrive

To stroke or drive the ball over the opponent's base line so that it lands outside of the playing court for an error.

Overhand

With the racket above the shoulder.

Overhead

A shot hit from a position higher than the player's head.

Overhead shot

A ball hit in the air above one's head, generally off a lob.

The Overhead Smash

Overhead smash

Crushing a ball with an overhead stroke into an area of the court so that the opponent cannot touch it or so that he finds it difficult or impossible to return the ball. Also called a 'smash' or 'kill'.

Overhitting

A player who tends to put too much force into each shot.

Overspin

Imparting a spin to the ball which makes the top of the ball rotate forwards along the same line that the ball is travelling. Also called 'top spin'.

P

Pace
The speed of the ball.

Padma Shri awardees
Winners
1. Ramanathan Krishnan,
2. Ghaus Mohammed Khan,
3. Raj Kumar Khanna,
4. Vijay Amritraj

Pakistan
Pakistan Lawn Tennis Association was founded in 1947, the year when Pakistan came into being, and affiliated to the I.L.T.F. in 1949. The most important championships staged by this association are the National Tennis Championships held in Lahore since 1949.

Palfrey, Miss Sarah
USA (born 1912) — A gifted volleyer and outstanding doubles player, she ranked US No. 4 in 1929, No. 1 in 1945. She renounced her amateur status in 1946.

Pan-American Championships
Tennis was included in the Pan-American games in Buenos Aires (1951).

Panatta, Adriano
Italy (born 1950) — The best Italian player since Nicola Pietrangeli,

Panatta enjoyed a fantastic year in 1976 when he won the Italian and French Open. He had always been dashing and stylish, but had never made full use of his talent.

Parallel formation

A positioning of players in a doubles game in which the partners keep abreast of each other on the court.

Parker, Frank

USA (born 1916) — One of America's most intelligent players though handicapped by lack of force on his forehand. He and Budge were mainly responsible for the American success in the Davis Cup against Great Britain in 1937. Became a professional in 1949.

Pass

To hit the ball past an opponent so that he cannot return it. Also a stroke that drives the ball past an opponent at the net, inside the court, but beyond his reach, as a passing shot.

Passing shot

The shot which passes beyond the reach of the net player and lands inbounds.

Pat-ball delivery

A soft service.

Patterson, Gerald L.

Australia (1895-1965) — A big Australian with a cannonball service and overpowering net attack, outstanding in the game after World War I. He came through Wimbledon in 1919 to overcome his compatriot Norman Brookes in the singles Challenge Round, lost his title to Tilden in the following year but came back in 1922 to become the first 'play through' champion at the new site of the All England Club. Wimbledon champion (singles) 1919, 1922; (mixed) 1920.

Patty, J. Edward

USA (born 1924) — An American who lived in Paris and developed his game there, 'Budge' Patty, with his elegant, effective forehand volley, was one of the great post-war stylists. He had beaten the Czech at Wimbledon in 1947 and 3 years later in his French final. He won the Italian singles 1954, and the German singles 1953/54 and doubles 1953/54/55.

Permanent fixtures

The umpire, linesmen, and spectators and their chairs or stands, net, posts, back and side stops, and any other objects situated around the court.

Perry, Frederick John

UK (born 1909) — He was the first British man to take all four Grand Slam singles titles. He won the US singles three times in 1933, 1934 and 1936, his only blemish being a semi-final loss to Wilmer Allison in 1935. He won the US mixed with Sarah Palfrey in 1932. He took the Australian singles and doubles (with Hughes) in 1934, and the French singles in 1935 and doubles (with Hughes) in 1933. And he led Great Britain to four successive victories in the Davis Cup 1933 to 1936.

Petra, Yvon Francois Marie

France (1916-1984) — Wimbledon's first post-war men's singles champion. Reached mixed final at Wimbledon 1937 with Simone Mathieu and won French doubles 1938 with Destremau, defeating Budge and Mako in final.

Philippines

The Philippine L.T.A. has been a full member of the I.L.T.F. since 1936. Its team first competed in the Davis Cup in 1926 and has a very good record.

Pietrangeli, Nicola

A player of superb touch, though never of consistency, he had a unique place in the annals of the game as the outstanding stalwart of the Davis Cup. Between 1954 and 1972 he played 164 Davis Cup rubbers for Italy, winning 119, this being 43 more than the rubbers played by the next on the list, Jacques Brichant of Belgium.

Pilic, Nicola

Yugoslavia (born 1939) — A tall left-hander. He was Wimbledon singles semi-finalist in 1967. He and Boro Jovanovic reached the Wimbledon doubles final in 1962, an achievement that was an ironic response to the exclusion that year of Yugoslavia from the European Zone of the Davis Cup on the grounds that they were not good enough. He became a contracted professional in 1968.

Place

To hit the ball accurately to a desired location on the court.

Placement

A stroke that places the ball beyond the reach of the opponent.

Platform tennis

This originates from a game known as Paddle tennis, played on the streets of New York with wooden 'paddles' and a sponge rubber ball.

Play

A warning called by the server just before serving. Also, the response of a linesman or umpire when appealed to for a decision on a ball that is good; an order to continue play.

Played

An abbreviation of "well played". Used as applause for a clever stroke. Also, the manner in which a ball is returned.

Players

Normally men play against men and women against women, except in mixed doubles, where opposing pairs each consist of a man and a woman.

Plugging the side line

A game strategy or tactic in which the player keeps playing his opponent's backhand until he is moved sufficiently out of position to be vulnerable for a forehand drop shot.

Poach

To hit a ball in doubles that should have been played by one's partner, usually applied to play at the net.

Point

The smallest unit of scoring. Four points scored win a game except when both sides have won three points, in which case the score is 'deuce' and the game continues until one player gains a lead of two clear points.

Point of impact

The point at which the racket meets the ball.

Porous Court (Pervious)

Is one which permits water to filter through the surface.

Position

Where a player stands in relation to the lines of the court, the net, the opponent, and the ball.

Position play

A strategy designed to manoeuvre the opponent out of position, placing the ball so that an opening is created.

Post

One of the wooden or metal uprights supporting the net.

Precision hitting

Clear clean-cut hitting off the centre of the racket.

Preliminary round

In tournament play, the first series of matches when the number of entries does not exactly equal a power of two. Same as first round.

Press

To attack, to force, to push. Also a device, once common, used to prevent warping of a tennis racket when not in use.

Price, Mrs. L.E.G.

S. Africa (born 1939) — A slender, graceful South African with a formidable forehand. She was Wimbledon singles finalist in 1960 and semifinalist in 1959 and 1961. She and Renee Schuurman formed a women's doubles partnership which, while short of the very best, came very near it.

Professional

One who receives pecuniary advantage by playing, teaching, demonstrating or pursuit of the game of tennis. There are two major classes: (1) Independent or registered professional — one who has reached the age of 18 years, accepts the authority of his national lawn tennis association at all times, and is authorized to derive pecuniary advantage from tennis; and (2) touring or contract professional — one who is under contract with an organization other than a national lawn tennis association or its affiliated bodies and who gains pecuniary advantage from taking part in events which are not organized by the national association of the country where they are held.

Put away

A shot hit so well that no return is made. Generally used when the shot is made off a weakish return.

Q

Quist, Adrian Karl

Australia (born 1913) — A shrewd, graceful doubles player, whose victories at Wimbledon were separated by a gap of 15 years. Won with J.H. Crawford in 1935 and, when almost a veteran, with J.E. Bromwich in 1950. Won 42 out of 55 Davis Cup rubbers in 28 ties between 1933-48.

R

Rackets

Rackets have wood or steel frames. A man's racket generally weighs 13(1/2)-14oz. (382.7g-396.9g) and a woman's 13-13(1/2)oz. (368.5g-382.7g).

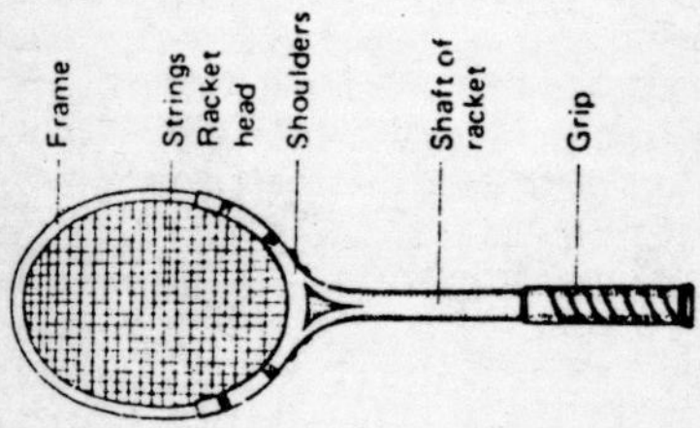

Rally

A prolonged series of shots with which the opponents keep the ball in play. In the early days of the game the term used was 'rest'.

Rallying

A prolonged series of strokes (ground-strokes and/or volleys). Also playing the ball to each other for practice or for warming up.

Ralston, R. Dennis

USA (born 1942) — Aggressive in game and originally aggressive in his personality. He made a striking Wimbledon debut in 1960 when he paired for the first time the Mexican Rafael Osuna and, after nearly being beaten in the first round, won the title. Ralston was only 17 years old.

Ranking

A list of players drawn up in order of ability. National lists are normally official, but international rankings are not.

Raw rubber ball

Latex (rubber) comes from the stems of certain trees. It was not until the 19th century that rubber-tree seeds were brought to Europe and grown commercially.

Reaching up and out

Making the service swing at the length of the arm and over the right (or left) shoulder.

Ready position

Classical posture in readiness to chase any ball and return it with an appropriate stroke: weight on toes, knees bent, body and mind alert for quick action.

Real failures (ball)

The traditional real tennis balls were made from sheepskin and filled with sawdust, sand or wool. They did not bounce on grass.

Real tennis

Real — or Royal — tennis used to be the sport of kings, and was a favourite pastime of the French and English monarchy. Henry VIII of England built a court at his Hampton Court place in the 16th century, and this is still used by real tennis enthusiasts today.

Receiver

The player about to return the opponent's serve.

Referee (organizer; arbiter)

The official in charge of a tournament.

Renshaw, William Charles

UK (1861-1904) — He won the Wimbledon singles 1881, 1882, 1883, 1884, 1885, 1886 and 1889, and the doubles in 1884, 1885, 1886, 1888, 1889. A major factor in converting tennis into an exciting spectacular sport.

Retire

To allow the opponent to win by with drawing before a match or by defaulting (discontinuing a match that has started).

Retrieve

Normally refers to a fine defensive shot in response to an opponent's well-placed offensive shot.

Retriever

A player whose style is primarily defensive and relies on running down and returning shots rather than putting away.

Return

To stroke the ball back over the net while in play.

Reverse twist

A stroke made by drawing the racket across the body in striking the ball.

Richey, Nancy Ann

USA (born 1942) — Later Mrs. Gunter. A Texan, famous for her shorts and peaked cap. She was, like her brother, George Clifford Richey, a tenacious baseliner, impressive on clay. Her determination occasionally brought unexpected success on grass. At Wimbledon she reached quarter-final seven times in nine years 1964-72 but was semi-finalist only in 1968. She won Wimbledon doubles with Maria Bueno in 1966.

Riggs, Bobby

USA (born 1918) — He won three events at Wimbledon 1939. Won USA singles in 1939 and turned professional in 1941. He was a champion of great guile. He assaulted opponents with a high-pitched chatter that must have sounded like squeaks to spectators. He launched an attack on the mind as well as on the body of his foe and rained confusion on both.

Roche, Tony

Australia (born 1945) — At Wimbledon he was runner-up in 1969 to Rod Laver, and he won the doubles five times with Newcombe — in 1965, 1968, 1969, 1970 and 1974. He took the mixed in 1976 with Francoise Durr. He was also runner-up in 1965 and 1969 with Judy Tagart. In the US singles he was runner-up in 1969 and 1970, and won the doubles with Newcombe in 1967. He won the French singles in 1966 over Istvan Gulyas of Hungary, having been runner-up the previous year to Fred Stolle.

Roland Garros

The stadium in Paris where the French Open is held.

Rosewall, Kenneth Robert

Australia (born 1934) — For a quarter of a century Rosewall's grace and easy, economical style delighted the connoisseurs and the only regret about his long and distinguished career is that, in spite of four finals over a period of 20 years, he never won the Wimbledon singles title. He began as a Hopman prodigy and it was not until the end of 1979 that he retired from Grand Prix tennis. In 1953, aged 18, he won the Australian and French singles and, with Hoad, the French and Wimbledon doubles.

Round

A specific series of matches in a tournament. The winners go forward to contest the next 'round'.

Round, Dorothy Edith

UK (born 1909) — She won Wimbledon women singles in 1934, 1937 and Australian singles 1935. She also won Wimbledon mixed doubles in 1934, 1935 and 1936.

Round robin

A method of playing a tournament by which each player meets all of the others in turn.

Rubber

A singles or doubles match in a team competition.

Rules

1. The court shall be a rectangle, 78 feet (23.77m.) long and 27 feet (8.23 m.) wide. It shall be divided across the middle by a net, suspended from a cord or metal cable of a maximum diameter of a third of an inch, the ends of which shall be attached to, or pass over the tops of two posts, 3 feet 6 inches (6.07m.) high, the centre of which shall be 3 feet (0.914) outside the court on each side. The height of the net shall be 3 feet (0.914 m.) at the centre, where it shall be held down taut by a strap not more than 2 inches (5 cm.) wide. There shall be a band covering the cord or metal cable and the top of the net for not less than 2 inches (5 cm.) nor more than 2½ inches (6.40 m.) in depth on each side. The lines bounding the ends and sides of the court shall respectively be called the base-lines and the side lines. On each side of the net, at a distance of 21 feet (6.40 m) from it and parallel with it, shall be drawn the service lines. The space on each side of the net between the service line and the side line shall be divided into two equal parts called the service courts by the centre service line, which must be 2 inches (5cm.) in width, drawn half-way between, and parallel with the side lines. Each base line shall be bisected by an imaginary continuation of the centre service line to a line 4 inches (10 cm.) in length and 2 inches (5 cm.) in width called the centre mark

drawn inside the court, at right angles to end in contact with such base lines. All other lines shall be not less than 1 inch (2.5 cm.) and not more than 2 inches (5 cm.) in width, except the base-line, which may be 4 inches (10 cm.) in width and all the measurements shall be made to the outside of the line.

NOTE — 1. In the case of International Lawn Tennis Championship (Davis Cup) or other Official Championships of the International Federation, there shall be a space behind each base line of not less than 21 feet (6.40 m), and at the sides of not less than 12 feet . (3.66 m.)

2. The permanent fixtures of the court shall include not only the net, posts, cord or metal cable, strap and band, but also, where there are any chairs around the court, and their occupants, all other fixtures around and above the court, and the umpire, foot-fault judge and linesman when in their respective places.

NOTE — For the purpose of this rule the word "umpire" comprehends the umpire and all those persons designated to assist him in the conduct of a match.

3. The ball shall have uniform outer surface. If there are any seams they shall be stitchless. The ball shall be more than two and a half inches and less than two and five-eight inches in diameter, and more than two ounces and less than two and one-sixteenth ounces in weight. The ball shall have a bound of more than 53 inches (153 cm.) and not less than 58 inches (147 cm.) when dropped 100 inches (254 cm.) upon a concrete base, and a deformation of more than 265 of an inch and less than 290 of an inch (.74 cm.) when subjected to a pressure of 18 lb. applied to each end of any diameter. All the tests for bound, size and deformation shall be made in accordance with the regulations in the official rule book.

4. The players shall stand on the opposite sides of the net; the player who first delivers the ball shall be called the server, and the other the receiver.

5. The choice of the sides and the right to be server or receiver in the first game shall be decided by toss. The player winning the toss

may choose or request his opponent to choose :-

(a) the right to be server or receiver, in which case the other player shall choose the side;

(b) the side, in which case the other player shall choose the right to be server or receiver.

6. The service shall be delivered in the following manner. Immediately before commencing to serve, the server shall with both feet at rest behind (i.e. further from the net than) the base line, and within the imaginary continuations of the centre-mark and side line. The server then shall project the ball by hand into the air in any direction and before it hits the ground strike it with his racket, and the delivery shall be deemed to have been completed at the moment of the impact of the racket and the ball. A player with the use of only one arm may utilize his racket for the projection.

7. The server shall throughout the delivery of the service :-

(a) not change his position by walking or running

(b) not touch, with either foot, any area other than that behind the base line within the imaginary extension of the centre mark and side line.

NOTE — The following interpretation of Rule 7 was approved by the International Federation on 9th July, 1958 :-

8. (a) The server shall not, by slight movements of the feet which do not materially affect the location originally taken up by him, be deemed "to change his position by walking or running"

(b) The word "foot" means the extremity of the leg below the ankle.

9. (a) In delivering the service, the server shall stand alternately behind the right and left courts, beginning from the right in every game. If service from a wrong half of the court occurs and is undetected, all play resulting from such wrong service or services shall stand, but the inaccuracy of station shall be corrected immediately if it is discovered.

(b) The ball served shall pass over the net and hit the ground within the service court which is diagonally opposite, or upon any line bounding such court, before the receiver returns it.

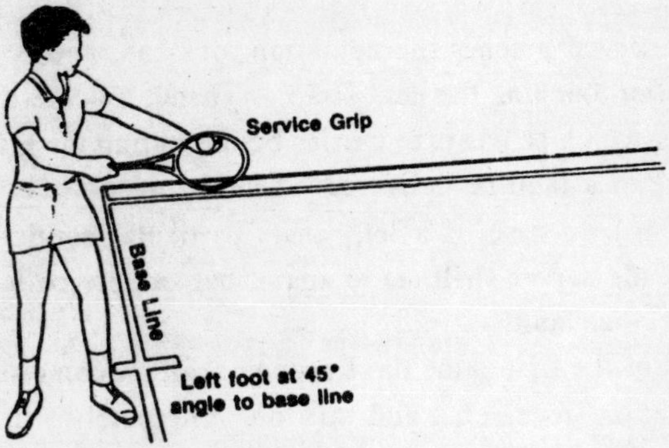

10. The service is a fault :

(a) if the server commits any breach of Rules 6, 7, or 8;

(b) if he misses the ball in attempting to strike it;

(c) if the ball served touches a permanent fixture (other than the net, strap or band) before it hits the ground.

11. After a fault (if it be the first fault) the server shall serve again from behind the same half of the court the wrong half, when in accordance with Rule 8, the server shall be entitled to one service only from behind the other half. A fault may not be claimed after the next service has been delivered.

12. The server shall not serve until the receiver is ready. If the latter attempts to return the service, he shall be deemed ready. If, however, the receiver signifies that he is not ready, he may not claim a fault because the ball does not hit the ground within the limits fixed for the service.

13. In all cases where a let has to be called under the rules, or to provide for an interruption of play, it shall have the following interpretations :-

(a) When called solely in respect of a service, that one service only shall be replayed.

(b) When called under any other circumstances, the point

shall be replayed.

14. The service is a let :-

(a) if the ball served touches the net, strap or band, and is otherwise good or after touching the net, strap or band, touches the receiver or anything which he wears or carries before hitting the ground.

(b) if a service or a fault be delivered when the receiver is not ready (see Rule 11). In case of a let, that particular service shall not count, and the server shall serve again, but a service let does not annul a previous fault.

15. At the end of the first game the Receiver shall become server, and the server the receiver; and so on alternately in all the subsequent games of a match. If a player serves out of turn, the player who ought to have served shall serve as soon as the mistake is discovered, but all the points scored before such discovery shall be reckoned. If a game shall have been completed before such discovery, the order or service remains as altered. A fault served before such discovery shall not be reckoned.

16. A ball is in play from the moment at which it is delivered in service. Unless a fault or a let be called it remains in play until the point is decided.

17. The server wins the point :-

(a) if the ball served, not being a let under Rule 13, touches the receiver or anything which he wears or carries, before it hits the ground;

(b) if the receiver otherwise loses the point as provided by Rule 18.

18. The receiver wins the point :-

(a) if the server serves two consecutive faults ;

(b) if the server otherwise loses the point as provided by rule 18.

19. A player loses the point if :-

(a) he fails, before the ball in play has hit the ground twice consecutively, to return it directly over the net except as provided in Rule 22 (a) or (c) ; or

(b) he returns the ball in play so that it hits the groun, a permanent fixture, or other object, outside any of the lines which bound his

opponent's court except as provided in Rule 22 (a) and (c); or

(c) he volleys the ball and fails to make a good return even when standing outside the court; or

(d) he touches or strikes the ball in play with his racket more than once in making a stroke; or

(e) he or his racket (in his hand or otherwise) or anything which he wears or carries touches the net, posts, cord or metal cable, strap or band, or the ground within his opponent's court at any time while the ball is in play; or

(f) he volleys the ball before it has passed the net; or

(g) the ball in play touches him or anything that he wears or carries, except his racket in his hand or hands; or

(h) he throws his racket and hits the ball.

20. If a player commits any act either deliberately or involuntarily which, in the opinion of the umpire, hinders the opponent in making a stroke, the umpire shall in the first case award the point to the opponent, and in the second case order the point to be replayed.

21. A ball falling on a line is regarded a falling in the court bounded by that line.

22. If the ball in play touches a permanent fixture (other than the net, posts, cord or metal cable, strap or band) after it has hit the ground,

the player who struck it wins the point; if before it hits the ground his opponent wins the point.

22. It is a good return :-

(a) If the ball touches the net, posts, cord or metal cable, strap or band, provided that it passes over any of them and hits the ground within the court; or

(b) If the ball, served or returned, hits the ground within the proper court and rebounds or be blown back over the net, and the player whose turn it is to strike reach over the net and play the ball, provided that neither he nor any part of his clothes or racket touches the net, posts, cord or metal cable, strap or band or the ground within his opponent's court, and that the stroke be otherwise good; or

(c) If the ball is returned outside the post, either above or below the level of the top of the net, even though it touches the post, provided that it hits the ground within the proper court; or

(b) If a player's racket passes over the net after he has returned the ball, provided the ball passes the net before being played and be properly returned; or

(e) If a player succeeds in returning the ball, served or in play, which strikes a ball laying in the court.

NOTE TO RULE 22 — In a singles match, if for the sake of convenience a doubles court be equipped with singles posts for the purpose of a singles game, then the doubles posts and those portions of the net, cord or metal cable and band outside such singles posts or parts of the net of a singles game.

A return that passes under the net cord between the singles and adjacent doubles post without touching either net cord, net or doubles post and falls within the area of play, is a good return.

23. In case a player is hindered in making a stroke by anything not within his control, except a permanent fixture of the court, or except as provided for in Rule 19, the point shall be replayed.

24. If a player wins his first point, the score is called 15 for that player; on winning his second point, the score is called 30 for that player;

on winning his third point, the score is called 40 for that player, and the fourth point won by a player is scored game for that player except as below:-

If both the players have won three points, the score is called deuce; and the next point won by a player is scored advantage for that player. If the same player wins the next, he wins the game; if the other player wins the next point the score is again called deuce; and so on, until a player wins the two points immediately following the score at deuce, when the game is scored for that player.

25. A player (or players) who first wins six games wins a set; except that he must win by a margin of two games over his opponent, and, where necessary, a set shall be extended until this margin be achieved.

26. The players shall change sides at the end of the first, third and every subsequent alternate game of each set, and at the end of each set unless the total number of games in such set be even, in which case the change is not made until the end of the first game of the next set.

27. The maximum number of sets in a match shall be 5, or where women take part, 3.

28. Except where otherwise stated, every reference in these Rules to the masculine includes the feminine gender.

29. Modified form of Law 29 according to International Lawn Tennis Federation, on 7th July, 1971.

In matches where an umpire is appointed, his decision shall be final; but where a referee is appointed, an appeal shall lie to him from the decision of an umpire on a question of law, and in all such cases the decision of the referee shall be final except that in Davis Cup matches the decision of a linesman can be changed by the referee, or by the umpire with the consent of the referee.

The referee, in his discretion, may at any time, postpone a match on account of darkness or the condition of the ground or the weather. In any case of postponement the previous score and previous occupancy of courts shall hold good, unless the referee and the players unanimously agree otherwise.

30. Play shall be continuous from the first service till the match be concluded; provided that after the third set, or when women take part, the second set, either player is entitled to a rest. Which shall not exceed 10 minutes, or in countries situated between Latitude 15 degrees North and Latitude 15 degrees South, 45 minutes, and provided further that when necessitated by circumstances not within the control of the players, the umpire may suspend play for such a period as he may consider necessary. If play be suspended and be not resumed until a later day the rest may be taken only after the third set (or when women take part, the second set) of play on such later day, completion of an unfinished set being counted as one set. These provisions shall be strictly construed, and play shall never be suspended, delayed or interfered with for the purpose of enabling a player to recover his strength or his mind, or to receive instruction or advice. The umpire shall be the sole judge of such suspension, delay or interference, and after giving due warning he may disqualify the offender.

Run back
The area between the base line and the court's backstop.

Runner-up
The loser in the final round of any tournament or event.

Running-in shot
A stroke made and followed to the net.

Rush
To advance to the net.

Rushing the net
A game strategy in which the player runs up close to the net after hitting the ball in hope that the opponent's return can be killed from this vantage spot.

Ryan, Elizabeth

USA (1892-1979) — Suzanne Lenglen's doubles partner and the winner of 19 Wimbledon titles — 12 doubles and 7 mixed. A determined competitor with a cunningly chopped forehand and a great appetite for match-play, she was regarded by contemporaries as 'the best player never to win a great singles championship'.

S

Sabatini, Gabriela

Argentina (born 1970) — When, as a 15-year-old, Gabriela Sabatini made history by becoming the youngest semi-finalist at the French Open, she couldn't speak to the press in English or French. It didn't matter because her conqueror, Chris Evert, said it all for her; "She's going to be a star". Four years later Evert's prediction is spot on. The 19-year-old Sabatini is nudging the No. 2 world ranking, is a millionaire and the sport's No. 1 pin-up girl. Argentina's heroine did her nation proud in Seoul by winning Argentina's first Olympic medal since 1972 — a silver for her runner-up effort against rival Steffi Graf. Carrying her country's flag onto the track at the opening ceremony was one of Sabatini's proudest moments.

Sangster, Michael J.

UK (born 1940) — Became the most successful British player for many years by virtue of a formidably fast service. He was singles semi-finalist at Wimbledon and Forest Hills in 1961, and in the French meeting in 1963. His delivery was timed in June 1963 at 154 m.p.h. He was the main strength behind Britain reaching the Inter-Zone finals of the Davis Cup in 1963. His 65 rubbers for Great Britain in the Davis Cup 1960 to 1968.

Schroeder, Frederick Rudolph

USA (born 1921) — A powerful Californian whose aggressive serve-and-volley game brought him much success on fast surfaces. The US National Junior Champion in 1939. A distinguished member of the US Davis Cup team between 1946 and 1951, he played in six challenge rounds, winning eight of his 11 singles and one of his four doubles.

Scoring

A tennis match is made up of sets and games. To win a set, a player must win six games. In most cases, a player wins the match by winning two out of three sets. However, players must sometimes win three out of five sets to win a match. A tennis game is won by scoring four points. In tennis, a score of zero is called love. The first point scored is called fifteen. The second point scored is called thirty, and the third point scored is called forty. The fourth and final point scored is called game, meaning that the game is over.

Second point

15-all, 30-love or love-30.

Seeding

A process by which the best or ranked entrants in a single elimination tournament are placed in the draw so that they will not meet each other in the early rounds of a tournament. The tournament committee, in effect, predicts the winner and seeds that player number one. The committee guesses who will be the second best player and seeds that person number two. Usually, for every eight entries, one player is seeded. The seeded players are then placed in specified positions in the draw. If the committee's predictions come true, the number one and number two seeded players will meet in the finals, and they will have defeated the number three and number four seeded players in the semifinals. Seedings are based on rankings and upon recent tournament performance. When a seeded player is defeated by an unseeded player, an upset has occurred.

Segura, Francisco

Ecuador (born 1921) — He had a double-fisted forehand of rare accuracy and power and his enthusiastic fighting qualities made him one of the most popular men in the professional ranks in the 1950s.

Seles, Monica

Yugoslavia (born 1973) — The 15-year-old Yugoslav phenomenon, who went from nowhere to No. 9 in the rankings in 1989, wrote her own formula.

Semifinal round

The round preceding the final round.

Semifinals

The two matches in the round before the finals; the matches of the semifinal round.

Serve

To deliver the ball from the base line by throwing it into the air with the hand and knocking it into the opponent's service court; the opening stroke of each point; the act of putting the ball into play.

Server

The player who serves.

Service

The action of serving corresponds with that of throwing a ball and, in teaching, professional coaches encourage pupils to 'throw your racket at the ball'. The first service of a game is made from the right-hand side of the court.

Theoretically, a person 6 feet 3 inches or more tall can, when reaching to full height with a racket, serve a ball that travels in a straight line to the spot where it bounces just within the service line. Players less tall must allow for the ball to dip in flight, either by reducing speed or by applying a spin which uses wind resistance to enforce the necessary dip.

Service ace

A point earned by serving a ball that cannot be returned.

The Advanced Service Swing

Service break

A game won by the receiver.

Service court

The space on either side of the net between the net and the service line. The centre line divides this area into two equal parts, the right (first) and left (second) service courts.

Service line

The line, 6.4m (21ft.) from the net, which bounds the length of each service court.

Service winner

A service which might be touched by the receiver but is not returned over the net.

Set

The unit of scoring next higher than the game; scored when either side has won six games, unless the other side has won five; in that case the side first gaining a lead of two games wins.

Setless

Without a set; when a player loses a match in "straight sets".

Set point

The point which, if won by the player holding it, seals the set.

Set point

See Match point.

Set-up

An easy return off which it is simple to win a point. Also called 'a sitter'.

Seventh point

Advantage server or Advantage receiver.

Shadow tennis

A practice procedure in footwork and strokes done without the use of a ball. Similar to shadow boxing performed by prize fighters.

Shag

To collect or retrieve idle balls knocked out of the court; the work of the ball boys.

Shamateurs

A term applied to players in the era of pre Open tennis (before 1968) who took 'under-the-counter' payments to compensate for the small prizes for playing in tournaments.

Shoes

The foot should have no room to move in a tennis shoe (blisters). For normal use in tennis, it is best to buy a fairly heavy, robust tennis shoe. The upper can be either of leather or canvas and must be provided with airholes. The sole must be well-shaped. The harder the ground on

which you play, the thicker the sole should be. Competition players need, in addition to training shoes, two pairs of lighter tennis shoes. After a game shoes must be left to dry out completely. New shoes should be worn in gradually.

Short ball

A ball lacking in depth which yields control of the rally to the opponent.

Shortest Wimbledon finals

In 1881, W. Renshaw defeated the Rev. J.T. Hartley 6-0, 6-1, 6-1 in 37 minutes for the men's singles title. Dorothea Lambert Chambers routed D.P. Boothby 6-0, 6-0, in 25 minutes in the women's final of 1911.

Shriver, Pam

USA (born 1962) — As a 16-year-old in 1978, Shriver stunned the tennis world by defeating Navratilova to become the youngest ever finalist at the US Open, but this remains her only appearance in a Grnd Slam singles final. Her doubles record with Navratilova is superlative. They won the Grand Slam in 1984 and were completely invincible for over two years, between April 1983 and July 1985. They have five Wimbledon titles (1981, 1982, 1983, 1984, 1986), four US titles (1983, 1984, 1986, 1987), six Australian (1982 to 1988 inclusive), four French (1984, 85, 1987, 88) and six Women's Series championships (1981, 1982, 1983, 1984, 1986, 1987).

Side line

The line running the full length of the court marking the outside limits of the playing court.

Side service line

The line forming the boundary of the service courts at the right and left sides. In singles the side service lines are also part of the side lines.

Sidespin

A ball hit and rotating on a horizontal plane.

Singles

A match in which one player opposes another player.

Singles sticks

Spiked sticks used when permanent posts support the net outside the doubles side lines. The sticks are 107 cm (42 in) high, they are pushed into the ground three feet outside the singles side lines and the net is hoisted on to them.

Sirola, Orlando

Italy (born 1928) — Tall Italian who formed a notable doubles partnership with Nicolo Pietrangeli. A strong and powerful player at his best he was extraordinarily unpredictable, having languid spells when he hardly seemed to try. He and Pietrangeli were doubles finalists in the French championships in 1955 and at Wimbledon in 1956.

Sixth point

Game or 40-40 (40-40 is called "deuce").

Slice

A slice puts backspin on the ball. (Backspin is a ball rotating in the air toward the person who hit it and away from the person who'll receive it.) This cause the ball either so "sit up" on the court or to break right or left of an opponent.

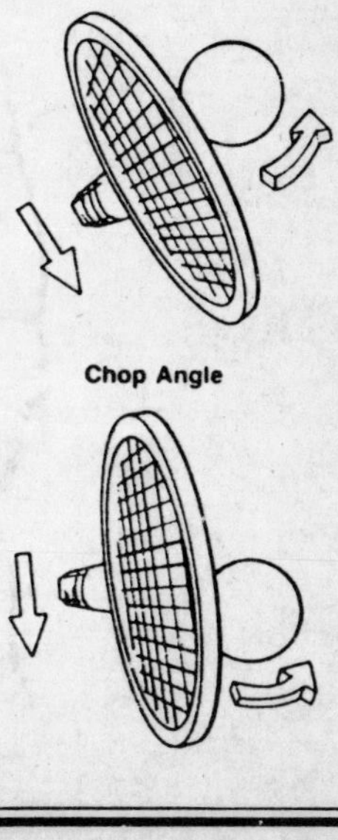

Slow court

Is one on which a moderately hard hit ball tends not to skid very much and the bounce is generally higher than on a fast court. A ball hit with spin may be diverted. Applies generally to rough surface courts.

Smash

A powerful overhead stroke played in response to a high ball, usually without letting the ball bounce. Often played near the net.

Smith, Stan

USA (born 1946) — At 26, Stan Smith has accomplished a great deal in tennis against history's better players and with more at stake. He began playing at 16, a late age by championship standards, and was junior champion two years later. He won the US Open in 1971, Wimbledon in 1972, the Grand Prix in 1971 and every Davis Cup singles match he has played. He wins when least expected. The best example was two straight-set victories over Ilie Nastase on clay when the Challenge Round outcome was in doubt. He won US National titles on all four surfaces — grass, clay, cement and indoors — including four US Open championships in 1968, 1974, 1978 and 1980. They were also runners-up in 1979, while at Wimbledon they reached the final in 1974 (the same year that they were runners-up in Paris), 1980 and 1981. They won the Australian title in 1970.

Space-age racket

The modern tennis racket is stronger and more powerful than ever before. Computers are used to help design the rackets, which are made from materials developed for the aerospace industry.

Spain

Spain challenged in the Davis Cup for the first time in 1920, relying upon her first major player. Alonso, an aggressive competitor, who had been taught the game by his English governess, and the Count de Gomar. She lost 4-1 to England at Hendon, but the following year beat India, reached the all-comers' final, and then in 1924 avenged her defeat by the English at Manchester and reached the final again.

Spain achieved little in postwar competition until the emergence of Gimeno, who turned professional in 1960 after winning 14 out of 22 rubbers.

Spikes
Shoes in which nails protude from the soles or heels to keep the player from slipping. Same as steel points.

Spin
A side, front, or back rotation of the ball caused by cutting the ball as it is hit.

Spinning
A method of determining which player serves first, and from which side

of the net. It is accomplished by one player spinning his racket rapidly and letting it fall to the ground. While the racket is spinning, the other player calls "rough" or "smooth," referring to the manner in which the trimming cord at the top and throat of the racket face is wound around the stringing.

Stolle, Frederick Sidney
Australia (born 1938) — He won French men's singles in 1965, USA singles in 1966. Shares with von Cramm the galling record of losing the Wimbledon singles final three years in succession (1963-65).

Stop volley
A volleying stroke intended to drop the ball barely over the net.

Straight sets
A match won without losing a set; setless.

Strap
A canvas strap in the centre of the net which is anchored to the ground to hold the net secure and at its proper height (3 feet at the centre). Also called centre strap and centre band.

Strategy
The general plan of play in a specific match usually based on the opponent's weaknesses. Also called game strategy.

Striker or striker-out
The player whose turn it is to return the service.

Stringing
The filament (animal gut, nylon, or silk) in the head of the racket.

Stroke
The action of hitting the ball with the racket.

Style
The manner in which a player strokes the ball. Also called form.

Sudden death
An expression meaning a set decided by one game, after the score has been even at five-all, in contradistinction to playing deuce-and-vantage sets.

Sweet spot
An area of the strings usually located slightly below the centre of the racket face. When the ball contacts the sweet spot, vibrations transmitted to the hand are minimal.

T

Tactics
The carrying out of the strategical plans; the ways and means used in the presence of the opponent.

Take the net
To move in close to the net.

Tape
The "band" of canvas bound on the top of the net. Also, the court line (derived from the occasional use of tapes for lines on clay courts).

Telegraphing the play
To indicate the direction of one's intended target before rotation of the ball at a 90 degree angle.

Tanner, Roscoe
USA (born 1951) — He beat Connors to reach the Wimbledon final in 1979 when he lost in five unforgettable sets to Borg. He took revenge in the US Open a couple of months later to deny the Swede yet another chance of the Grand Slam. Unkindly referred to a player with a serve looking for a game to go with it.

Tennis
Presumably derived from the French verb tenez, the imperative of tenir, which means to hold, take, or receive. Thus, the name of the game is inherent in the rules which require that the server must hold the attention of the receiver before the serve may be legally delivered.

Tennis elbow
An inflammation and swelling of the elbow joint, resulting from too much playing.

Tennis leg
A rupture of some of the muscle fibers in the calf of the leg, resulting from a sudden twist or strain.

Tennis stroke
A stroke made by cutting or slicing the ball under so that it twists backward. Same as cut stroke.

Thailand
Thailand was first affiliated to the I.L.T.F. as an associate member in 1952, became a full member in 1962 but agreed to be an associate member again in 1971.

Third point
15-30, 30-15, 40-love, or love-40.

Thirty
A term used in scoring to denote two points. Also, in handicap matches, two points given on every game.

Thirty-all
A term used in scoring to denote that each side has scored two points.

Three-handed tennis
A form of practice in which one player, wishing to sharpen his reflexes, is faced by two opponents. As soon as one ball is dead another is hit towards the single player.

Three (or two) straight
A match won in successive sets; a setless victory. Same as straight sets.

Throat

The part of a tennis racket between the head and the handle.

Tie-breaker

A means of resolving sets that have reached a certain stage (6-all or 8-all, for example).

Tilden, William Tatem

USA (1893-1953) — He had every shot in the book, including a cannonball service, an acute command of tactics and a fine match temperament. He reigned undisputed king of the American game from 1920 to 1925 and came back to win Wimbledon for the third time in 1930 at the age of 37. Among his impressive achievement was his record in the Davis Cup. He won 13 successive singles in the Challenge Round between 1920 and 1926.

Todd, Mrs. P.C.

USA (born 1922) — A player of statuesque grace, she suffered from being the contemporary of Louise Bough, Margaret Dupont and Doris Hart. She won Wimbledon women's doubles in 1947.

TOP SPIN

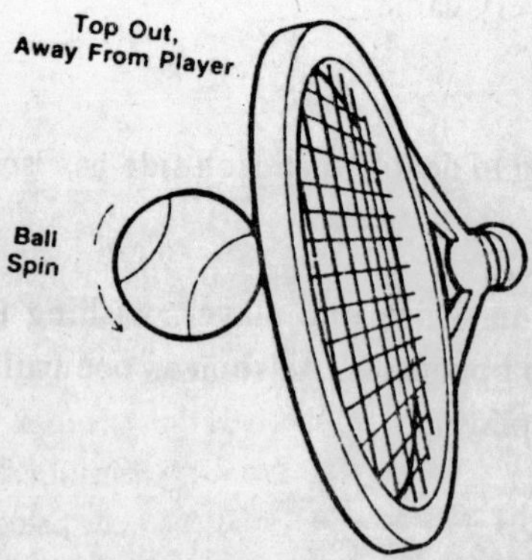

Top

To hit the ball on top, causing it to spin downward; the ball tends to bounce backward when it hits the ground.

Top spin

A stroke which imparts forward rotation to the ball. The ball dips in flight; the shot is used extensively to pass opponent attacking at the net.

Toss

A method to determine which player serves first, and from which side of the net. This is usually accomplished by spinning a racket and the player who wins the toss has his choice of serving or receiving, or the choice of side. He cannot choose both. Also throwing a ball into the air to start a serve.

Toss the racket (Spin the racket)

At the beginning of a match, a racket is "tossed" so that it lands flat on the ground. Formerly the terms rough and smooth were used in calling the toss; the winner (and the loser) of the toss make certain choices.

Touch

The ability to make delicate soft shots from several positions on the court.

Tournament

An official competition.

Trabert, Tony

USA (born 1930) — Trabert's sports career was channelled to tennis by fellow Ohioan Bill Talbert. Talbert nurtured his protege, and in 1950, when Trabert was only 19, the pair won a number of successive doubles matches, including the Italian and French Nationals. In 1955, he was the champion of the world, capturing the Wimbledon, the US and French Championships, the US Indoors and the US Clay Courts. Never before had anyone shown such virtuosity on as wide a variety of surfaces.

Trajectory

Refers to ball flight which is caused by the method of stroke production (2, 3). Understanding various trajectories and their attributes plays an important role in strategy and in making the correct choice of shots.

Tramline

The area between the singles and doubles side lines.

Truman, Christine

UK (born 1941) — After languishing in the shadow of the all-conquering Americans for 20 years, Britain suddenly produced a crop of champions in the late 1950s of which Truman was the youngest and most naturally talented. Angela Buxton, Angela Mortimer, Shirley Bloomer (later Mrs. Brasher) and Pat Ward had all made their mark by the time Truman burst upon the scene in 1957. The bouncy 16-year-old romped through the first three rounds at her first Wimbledon, then stunned the pundits by trouncing third-seeded Bloomer, the reigning French champion, to reach the quarter-finals. She then survived a gruelling three-set match against a second-rank American, Betty Pratt, to line up in the semi-finals against the favourite Althea Gibson.

Turbull, Wendy

Australia (born 1952) — Australian Sports Personality of the year in 1979, she had a doubles record that season with Betty Stove of 50 wins and just three losses as they collected the US Open, French and Italian titles.

Twist

A special rotation imparted to the ball during the serve causing the ball to jump to the left (or right-handed server).

Two step

Step-together-step. A movement commonly used to make small adjustments in position. When moving to the right, make the first step with the right foot, bring the left foot up to it, and then step again on the right foot.

U

Umpire

A man or woman in charge of a match, normally seated in a high chair by the net post. At important events linesmen and net-cord judges assist the umpire.

Undercut

A stroke made with the racket below the level of the shoulders.

Underhand

Hit the ball by bringing the hand forward and up from below the shoulders.

Underspin

A counterclockwise spin placed on the ball by catching the back side and bottom side of the ball with the racket head.

Up

An equal score; used as all.

U.S.A.

The first British experiments in Lawn Tennis were followed quickly by the introduction of the game to the United States. In 1874 Dr. Dwight and F.R. Sears, the elder brother of Richard Sears, the first U.S. singles champion, were playing on a court at Nahant.

USA Open Tournament

An American championship, open to all comers, was held at Staten Island in September 1880 and won by Englishman O.E. Woodhouse. In 1881, the first men's singles and men's doubles championships were contested at Newport. In 1915 both singles competitions were transferred to the Westside Lawn Tennis Club, Forest Hills, New York.

Men's Singles

1881	Richard Sears	USA
1882	Richard Sears	USA
1883	Richard Sears	USA
1884	Richard Sears	USA
1885	Richard Sears	USA
1886	Richard Sears	USA
1887	Richard Sears	USA
1888	Henry Slocum Jr	USA
1889	Henry Slocum Jr	USA
1890	Oliver Campbell	USA
1891	Oliver Campbell	USA
1892	Oliver Campbell	USA
1893	Robert Wrenn	USA
1894	Robert Wrenn	USA
1895	Fred Hovey	USA
1896	Robert Wrenn	USA
1897	Robert Wrenn	USA
1898	Malcolm Whitman	USA
1899	Malcolm Whitman	USA
1900	Malcolm Whitman	USA
1901	William Larned	USA

1902	William Larned	USA
1903	Lawrence Doherty	UK
1904	Holcombe Ward	USA
1905	Beals Wright	USA
1906	William Clothier	USA
1907	William Larned	USA
1908	William Larned	USA
1909	William Larned	USA
1910	William Larned	USA
1911	William Larned	USA
1912	Maurice McLoughlin	USA
1913	Maurice McLoughlin	USA
1914	Norris Williams	USA
1915	William Johnston	USA
1916	Norris Williams	USA
1917	Lindley Murray	USA
1918	Lindley Murray	USA
1919	W.M. Johnston	USA
1920	Bill Tiden	USA
1921	Bill Tiden	USA
1922	Bill Tiden	USA
1923	Bill Tiden	USA
1924	Bill Tiden	USA
1925	Bill Tiden	USA
1926	Rene Lacoste	Fra
1927	Rene Lacoste	Fra
1928	Henri Cochet	Fra
1929	Bill Tiden	USA
1930	John Doeg	USA
1931	H. Ellsworth Vines	USA
1932	H. Ellsworth Vines	USA
1933	Fred Perry	UK
1934	Fred Perry	UK
1935	Wilmer Allison	USA

1936	Fred Perry	UK
1937	Don Budge	USA
1938	Don Budge	USA
1939	Robert Riggs	USA
1940	Don McNeil	USA
1941	Robert Riggs	USA
1942	F.R. Schroeder Jr.	USA
1943	Joseph Hunt	USA
1944	Frank Parker	USA
1945	Frank Parker	USA
1946	Jack Kramer	USA
1947	Jack Kramer	USA
1948	Pancho Gonzales	USA
1949	Pancho Gonzales	USA
1950	Arthur Larsen	USA
1951	Frank Sedgman	Aus
1952	Frank Sedgman	Aus
1953	Tony Trabert	USA
1954	E.Victor Seixas Jr	USA
1955	Tony Trabert	USA
1956	Ken Rosewall	Aus
1957	Malcolm Anderson	Aus
1958	Ashley Cooper	Aus
1960	Neale A. Fraser	Aus
1961	Neale A. Fraser	Aus
1962	Rod Laver	Aus
1963	Rafael Osuna	Mex
1964	Roy Emerson	Aus
1965	Manuel Santana	Spa
1966	Fred Stolle	Aus
1967	John Newcombe	Aus
1968	Arthur Ashe	USA
1969	Rod Laver	Aus
1970	Ken Rosewall	Aus

1971	Stan Smith	USA
1972	Ilie Nastase	Rom
1973	John Newcombe	Aus
1974	Jimmy Connors	USA
1975	Manuel Orantes	Spa
1976	Jimmy Connors	USA
1977	Guillermo Vilas	Arg
1978	Jimmy Connors	USA
1979	John McEnroe	USA
1980	John McEnroe	USA
1981	John McEnroe	USA
1982	Jimmy Connors	USA
1983	Jimmy Connors	USA
1984	John McEnroe	USA
1985	Ivan Lendl	Cz
1986	Ivan Lendl	Cz
1987	Ivan Lendl	Cz
1988	Mats Wilander	Swe
1989	Boris Becker	W.Ger

Women's Singles

1887	Ellen Hansell	USA
1888	Bertha Townsend	USA
1889	Bertha Townsend	USA
1890	Ellen Roosevelt	USA
1891	Mabel Cahill	USA
1892	Mabel Cahill	USA
1893	Aline Terry	USA
1894	Helen Helwig	USA
1895	Juliette Atkinson	USA
1896	Elisabeth Moore	USA
1897	Juliette Atkinson	USA
1898	Juliette Atkinson	USA
1899	Marion Jones	USA

1900	Myrtle McAteer	USA
1901	Elisabeth Moore	USA
1902	Marion Jones	USA
1903	Elisabeth Moore	USA
1904	May Sutton	USA
1905	Elisabeth Moore	USA
1906	Helen Homans	USA
1907	Evelyn Sears	USA
1908	Maud Bargar-Wallach	USA
1909	Hazel Hotchkiss	USA
1910	Hazel Hotchkiss	USA
1911	Hazel Hotchkiss	USA
1912	Mary Browne	USA
1913	Mary Browne	USA
1914	Mary Browne	USA
1915	Molla Bjurstedt	USA
1916	Molla Bjurstedt	USA
1917	Molla Bjurstedt	USA
1918	Molla Bjurstedt	USA
1919	Wightman	USA
1920	Mallory	USA
1921	M. Mallory	USA
1922	M. Mallory	USA
1923	Wills	USA
1924	Wills	USA
1925	Wills	USA
1926	Mallory	USA
1927	Wills	USA
1928	Wills	USA
1929	Wills	USA
1930	Nuthall	UK
1931	Moody	USA
1932	Helen Jacobs	USA
1933	Helen Jacobs	USA

1934	Helen Jacobs	USA
1935	Helen Jacobs	USA
1936	Alice Marble	USA
1937	Anita Lizana	Chi
1938	Alice Marble	USA
1939	Alice Marble	USA
1940	Alice Marble	USA
1941	Sarah P. Cooke	USA
1942	Pauline Betz	USA
1943	Pauline Betz	USA
1944	Pauline Betz	USA
1945	Sarah P. Cooke	USA
1946	Pauline Betz	USA
1947	A. Louise Brough	USA
1948	Margaret O. duPont	USA
1949	Margaret O. duPont	USA
1950	Margaret O. duPont	USA
1951	Maureen Connolly	USA
1952	Maureen Connolly	USA
1953	Maureen Connolly	USA
1954	Doris Hart	USA
1955	Doris Hart	USA
1956	Shirley J. Fry	USA
1957	Althea Gibson	USA
1958	Althea Gibson	USA
1959	Maria Bueno	Bra
1960	Darlene Hard	USA
1961	Darlene Hard	USA
1962	Margaret Smith	Aus
1963	Maria Bueno	Bra
1964	Maria Bueno	Bra
1965	Margaret Smith	USA
1966	Maria Bueno	Bra
1967	Billie Jean King	USA

1968	Virginia Wade	UK
1969	Margaret Smith Court	Aus
1970	Margaret Smith Court	Aus
1971	Billie Jean King	USA
1972	Billie Jean King	USA
1973	Margaret Smith Court	Aus
1974	Billie Jean King	USA
1975	Chris Evert	USA
1976	Chris Evert	USA
1977	Chris Evert	USA
1978	Chris Evert	USA
1979	Tracy Austin	USA
1980	Chris Evert Lloyd	USA
1981	Tracy Austin	USA
1982	Chris Evert Lloyd	USA
1983	Martina Navratilova	USA
1984	Martina Navratilova	USA
1985	Hana Mandlikova	Cz
1986	Martina Navratilova	USA
1987	Martina Navratilova	USA
1988	Steffi Graf	W. Ger
1989	Steffi Graf	W. Ger

Men's Doubles

1919	N.E. Brookes, G.L. Patterson	Aus
1920	W.M. Johnston, C.J. Griffin	USA
1921	Bill Tilden, Vincent Richards	USA
1922	Bill Tilden, Vincent Richards	USA
1923	Bill Tilden, Brian Norton	SAf
1924	Howard Kinsey, Robert Kinsey	USA
1925	R. Norris Williams, Vincent Richards	USA
1926	R. Norris Williams, Vincent Richards	USA
1927	Bill Tilden, Francis Hunter	USA
1928	George Lott, John Hennessey	USA

1929	George Lott, John Doeg	USA
1930	George Lott, John Doeg	USA
1931	Wilmer Allison, John Van Ryn	USA
1932	H. Ellsworth Vinces, Keith Gledhill	USA
1933	George Lott, Lestr Stoefen	USA
1934	George Lott, Lestr Stoefen	USA
1935	Wilmer Allison, John Van Ryn	USA
1936	Don Budge, C. Gene Mako	USA
1937	Baron G. von Carmm, Henner Henkel	Ger
1938	Don Budge, C. Gene Mako	USA
1939	Adrian Quist, John Bromwich	Aus
1940	Jack Kramer, Frederick Schroeder Jr.	USA
1941	Jack Kramer, Frederick Schroeder	USA
1942	Gardner Mulloy, William Talbert	USA
1943	Jack Kramer, Frank Parker	USA
1944	Don McNeill, Robert Falkenburg	USA
1945	Gardner Mulloy, William Talbert	USA
1946	Gardner Mulloy, William Talbert	USA
1947	Jack Kramer, Frederick Schroeder Jr.	USA
1948	Gardner Mulloy, William Talbert	USA
1949	John Bromwich, William Sidwell	Aus
1950	John Bromwich, Frank Sedgman	Aus
1951	Frank Sedgman, Kenneth McGregor	Aus
1952	Mervyn Rose, E. Victor Seixas Jr.	USA
1953	Rex Hartwig, Mervyn Rose	Aus
1954	E. Victor Seixas Jr, Tony Trabert	USA
1955	Kosel Kamo, Atsushi Miyagi	Jpn
1956	Lewis Hoad, Ken Rosewall	Aus
1957	Ashley Cooper, Neale Fraser	Aus
1958	Hamilton Richardson, Alejandro Olmedo	USA
1959	Neale A. Fraser, Roy Emerson	Aus
1960	Neale A. Fraser, Roy Emerson	Aus
1961	Dennis Ralston, Chuck McKingley	USA
1962	Rafael Osuna, Antonio Palafox	Mex

1963	Dennis Ralston, Chuck McKinley	USA
1964	Dennis Ralston, Chuck McKinley	USA
1965	Roy Emerson, Fred Stolle	Aus
1966	Roy Emerson, Fred Stolle	Aus
1967	John Newcombe, Tony Roche	Aus
1968	Robert Lutz, Stan Smith	USA
1969	K.R. Rosewall, F.S. Stolle	Aus
1970	Pierre Barthes, Nicki Pilic	Yug
1971	John Newcombe, Roger Taylor	UK
1972	Chiff Darysdale, Roger Taylor	UK
1973	John Newcombe, Owen Davidson	Aus
1974	Bob Lutz, Stan Smith	USA
1975	Jimmy Connors, Ilie Nastase	Rom
1976	Marty Riessen, Tom Okker	USA
1977	Bob Hewitt, Frew McMillan	SAf
1978	Stan Smith, Bob Lutz	USA
1979	John McEnroe, Peter Fleming	USA
1980	Stan Smith, Bob Lutz	USA
1981	John McEnroe, Peter Fleming	USA
1982	Kevin Curren, Steve Denton	USA
1983	John McEnroe, Peter Fleming	USA
1984	John Fitzgerald, Tomas Smid	Cz
1985	Ken Flach, Robert Seguro	USA
1986	Andres Gomez, Slobodan Zivolnovic	Yug
1987	Stefan Edberg, Anders Jarryd	Swe
1988	Sergio Csal, Emilio Sanchez	Spa
1989	John McEnroe (USA), Mark Woodforde	Aus

Women's Doubles

1919	E.E. Goss, M. Zinderstein	USA
1920	E.E. Goss, M. Zinderstein	USA
1921	M.K. Browne, L.Williams	USA
1922	M. Jessup (nee Zinderstein), H.N. Wills	USA
1923	P. Covell (nee Howkins), K. Mckane	UK

1924	H.V.Wightman (nee Howkins), K. McKane	UK
1925	M.K. Browne, H.N.Wills	USA
1926	E.E. Goss, E. Ryan	USA
1927	K.Godfree (nee McKane), E.H. Harvey	UK
1928	H.V.Wightman (nee Hotchkiss), H.N.Wills	USA
1929	P. Michel (nee Saunders), P.H.Watson	UK
1930	B. Nuthall (UK), S. Palfrey	USA
1931	B. Nuthall, E. Whittingstall (nee Bennett)	UK
1932	H.H. Jacobs, B. Nuthall	UK
1933	F. James, B. Nuthall	UK
1934	H.H. Jacobs, S. Palfrey	USA
1935	H.H. Jacobs, S. Fabyan (nee Gladman)	USA
1936	M.G. Van Ryn, Carolin Babcock	USA
1937	Sarah P. Fabyan, Alice Marble	USA
1938	Alice Marble, Mrs. Sarah P. Fabyan	USA
1939	Alice Marble, Mrs. Sarah P. Fabyan	USA
1940	Alice Marble, Mrs. Sarah P. Fabyan	USA
1941	S.P. Cooke, Margaret Osborne	USA
1942	A.Louise Brough, Margaret Oborne	USA
1943	A. Louise Brough, Margaret Oborne	USA
1944	A. Louise Brough, Margaret Oborne	USA
1945	A. Louise Brough, Margaret Oborne	USA
1946	A. Louise Brough, Margaret Oborne	USA
1947	A. Louise Brough, Margaret Oborne	USA
1948	A. Louise Brough, Mrs. M.O. duPont	USA
1949	A. Louise Brough, Mrs. M.O. duPont	USA
1950	A. Louise Brough, Mrs. M.O. duPont	USA
1951	Doris Hart, Shirley Fry	USA
1952	Doris Hart, Shirley Fry	USA
1953	Doris Hart, Shirley Fry	USA
1954	Doris Hart, Shirley Fry	USA
1955	A. Louise Brough, Mrs. M.O. duPont	USA
1956	A. Louise Brough, Mrs. M.O. duPont	USA
1957	A. Louise Brough, Mrs. M.O. duPont	USA

	USA
1958 Darlene Hard, Jeanne Arth	USA
1959 Darlene Hard, Jeanne Arth	USA
1960 Darlene Hard (USA), Maria Bueno	Bra
1961 Darlene Hard (USA), Lesley Turner	Aus
1962 Maria Bueno (Bra), Darlene Hard	USA
1963 Margaret Smith, Robyn Ebbern	Aus
1964 Billie Jean Moffitt, Karen Susman	USA
1966 M.E. Bueno (Bra), Nancy Richey	USA
1967 Rosemary Casals, Bilie Jean King	USA
1968 M.E.Bueno (Bra), M.Court	Aus
1969 Francoise Durr (Fra), Darlene Hard	USA
1970 M.S. Court, Judy Tegart Dalton	Aus
1971 Rosemary Casals (USA), J. Tegart Dalton	Aus
1972 Francoise Durr (Fra), Betty Stove	Neth
1973 Margaret S. Court (Aus), Virginia Wade	UK
1974 Billie Jean King, Rosemary Casals	USA
1975 Margaret Court (Aus), Virginia Wade	UK
1976 Linky Boshoff, Ilana Kloss	SAf
1977 Betty Stove (Neth), Martina Navratilova	Cz
1978 Martina Navratilova (Cz), Billie Jean King	USA
1979 Betty Stove (Neth), Wendy Turnbull	Aus
1980 Martina Navratilova (Cz), Billie Jean King	USA
1981 Kathy Jordan, Anne Smith	USA
1982 Rosemary Casals (USA), Wendy Turnbull	Aus
1983 Martina Navratilova, Pam Shriver	USA
1984 Martina Navratilova, Pam Shriver	USA
1985 Claudia Kohde-Kilsch (W.Ger), Helena Sukova	Cz
1986 Martina Navratilova, Pam Shriver	USA
1987 Martina Navratilova, Pam Shriver	USA
1988 Gigi Fernandez (P.Rico), Robin White	USA
1989 Martina Navratilova (USA), Hana Mandlikova	Aus

Mixed Doubles

1943	William Talbert, Margaret Osborne	USA
1944	William Talbert, Margaret Osborne	USA
1945	William Talbert, Margaret Osborne	USA
1946	William Talbert, Margaret Osborne	USA
1947	John Bromwich (Aus), Louise Brough	USA
1948	Tom Brown, Louise Brough	USA
1949	Eric Sturgess (SAf), Louise Brough	USA
1950	Ken McGregor (Aus), Margaret DuPont	USA
1951	Frank Sedgman (Aus), Doris Hart	USA
1952	Frank Sedgman (Aus), Doris Hart	USA
1953	Vic Seixas, Doris Hart	USA
1954	Vic Seixas, Doris Hart	USA
1955	Vic Seixas, Doris Hart	USA
1956	Ken Rosewall (Aus), Margaret Du Pont	USA
1957	Kurt Nielsen (Den), Althea Gibson	USA
1958	Neale Fraser (Aus), Margaret DuPont	USA
1959	Neale Fraser (Aus), Margaret DuPont	USA
1960	Neale Fraser (Aus), Margaret DuPont	USA
1961	Robert Mark, Margaret Smith	Aus
1962	Fred Stolle, Margaret Smith	Aus
1963	Ken Fletcher, Margaret Smith	Aus
1964	John Newcombe, Margaret Smith	Aus
1965	Fred Stolle, Margaret Smith	Aus
1966	Owen Davidson (Aus), Donna Fales	USA
1967	Owen Davidson (Aus), Billie Jean King	USA
1968	Peter Curtis (UK), Mary-Ann Eisel	USA
1969	Paul Sullivan, Patty Hogan	USA
1970	Marty Riessen (USA), Margaret Court	Aus
1971	Owen Davidson (Aus), Billie Jean King	USA
1972	Marty Riessen (USA), Margaret Court	Aus
1973	Owen Davidson (Aus), Billie Jean King	USA
1974	Geoff Masters (Aus), Pam Teeguarden	USA
1975	Dick Stodcdkton, Rosemary Casals	USA

1976	Phil Dent (Aus), Billie Jean King	USA
1977	Frew McMillan (S. Af), Betty Stove	Hol
1978	Frew McMillan (S. Af), Betty Stove	Hol
1979	Bob Hewitt, Greer Stevens	S.Af
1980	Marty Riessen, Wendy Turnbull	USA
1981	Kevin Curren (S. Af), Anne Smith	USA
1982	Kevin Curren (S. Af), Anne Smith	USA
1983	John Fitzgerald, Elizabeth Sayers	Aus
1984	Tom Gullikson (USA), Manuela Maleeva	Bul
1985	Heinz Gunthardt (Swi), Martina Navratilova	USA
1986	Sergio Casal (Spa), Raffaella Reggi	Ita
1987	Emilio Sanchez (Spa), Raffaella Reggi	Ita
1988	Jim Pugh (USA), Jana Novotna	Cz
1989	Shelby Cannon, Robin White	USA

U.S.L.T.A.

Abbreviation for the United States Lawn Tennis Association.

U.S.P.T.A.

The United States Professional Tennis Association. An organization for teaching professionals (more than 2800 certified members) designed to promote ethical standards and sound educational method in tennis teaching.

U.S.S.R.

The Lawn Tennis Federation of the USSR was founded in 1922 and affiliated to the I.L.T.F. in 1956; since then a dramatic improvement has been made in the development and standard of play. Today there are over 1000 clubs in the USSR with more than 80,000 active players.

U.S.T.A.

The United States Tennis Association. Formerly the U.S.L.T.A.

V

V.A.S.S.S.
Van Alen Simplified Scoring System.

Van Dillen, Erik
USA (born 1951) — Played key minor role in famous US Davis Cup final in 1972 v Rumania when, with Smith, he won doubles against Nastase and Tiriac.

Vantage
The score of a game after either side has won a point from "deuce". Same as advantage.

Vantage-all
A term used in scoring, when the usual method of deuce-and-vantage games or sets is not used. When the best two out of three points (for games) or games (for sets) decide the game or set, the score is vantage-all when each side has won one point or games after deuce.

Vantage game
The next game won by either side in a deuce-and-vantage set, after the score of games has been at deuce.

Vantage-in
A term used to indicate that the server has won the "vantage" point (opposite of "vantage-out"). Same as vantage-server.

Vantage out

A term indicating that the receiver won the next point after deuce. Also called 'vantage striker' or 'vantage receiver'.

Vantage sets

Sets in which deuce-and-vantage has been or is to be played.

Veteran

A player over (men) 45 years of age; (women) 40 years of age. Same as senior player.

Vilas, Guillermo

Argentina (born 1952) — He has maintained a place in the top ten since 1974 when he captured the Masters on the grass at Melbourne. His best year was 1977 when he won the French and US Opens and strung together a 50-match winning streak. He lost his top ranking in Argentina to his great rival Jose-Luis Clerc in 1981, the year they combined to win the Davis Cup.

Vines, H. Ellsworth

USA (born 1911) — He won USA singles 1931, 1932 and Wimbledon singles 1932.

Virginia Slims/Avon Series

From 1971 there was an annual series of Virginia Slims tournaments, with a Championships as the climax. Avon Products took over the sponsorship from 1979-82.

Singles

1971	Billie Jean King	USA
1972	Chris Evert	USA
1973	Chris Evert	USA
1974	Evonne Goolagong	Aus
1975	Chris Evert	USA
1976	Evonne Cawley	Aus

1977	Chris Evert	USA
1978	Martina Navratilova	Cz
1979	Martina Navratilova	Cz
1980	Tracy Austin	USA
1981	Martina Navratilova	Cz
1982	Sylvia Hanika	FRG
1983	Martina Navratilova	USA
1984	Martina Navratilova	USA
1985	Martina Navratilova	USA
1986	Martina Navratilova	USA
1987	Steffi Graf	W.Ger
1988	Gabriela Sabatini	Arg
1989	Steffi Graf	W. Ger

Doubles

1971	Rosemary Casals, Bille Jean King	USA
1973	Rosemary Casals, Margaret Court	Aus
1974	Rosemary Casals, Billie Jean King	USA
1979	Francoise Durr (Fra), Betty Stove	Hol
1980	Billie Jean King (USA), Martina Navratilova	Cz
1981	Martina Navratilova (Cz), Pam Shriver	USA
1982	Martina Navratilova, Pam Shriver	USA
1984	Martina Navratilova, Pam Shriver	USA
1985	Hana Mandlikova (Cz), Wendy Turnbull	Aus
1986	Martina Navratilova, Pam Shriver	USA
1987	Martina Navratilova, Pam Shriver	USA
1988	Martina Navratilova, Pam Shriver	USA
1989	Martina Navratilova, Pam Shriver	USA

V.I.T.A.

The Veteran International Tennis Association was founded in 1956 as the international governing body for veterans (seniors) and is recognized by the I.L.T.F.

Volley

They are usually made from positions near to the net, they are essentially aggressive; there is no time for a full swing but the volleyer is positioned dangerously so he must try to end the rally immediately. This usually involves a shortened movement which is likened by coaches to everyday actions by the words 'punch your volleys'.

Volleyer

A player who uses the "net game"; one who volleys by preference (opposite to a base line player).

Von Cramm, Baron Gottfried

Germany (born 1909) — Played with classical and fluent precision. Like Fred Stolle in later years, was Wimbledon finalist three years running 1935 to 1937, losing twice to Fred Parry and then to Don Budge. Perry's victory over him in 1936 by 6-1, 6-1, 6-0 was the most one-sided ever but Von Cramm was loath to give himself an alibi because of an injured ankle.

W

W.C.T.

World Championship of Tennis Inc., a major promotional organization with many activities of which their W.C.T. Championships are the most prominent.

W.I.T.A.

Women's International Tennis Association, a rival to the W.T.A.

W.T.A.

Women's Tennis Association. The female equivalent of the A.T.P.

W.T.T.

World Team Tennis Inc. An American company which promotes inter-city league tennis.

Wade, Sarah Virginia

UK (born 1945) — Strong and athletic, she had a powerful service, though it was not a fluid stroke. A sliced backhand, adequate fore-hand, good overhead and crisp volleys became much better once she learned not to snatch them. In 1974 Wimbledon she was a semi-finalist for the first time, and frittered away a winning lead against Russia's Olga Morozova, and she was well beaten by Goolagong in the semi-finals of 1976. She won the US Open doubles with Margaret Court in 1973 and 1975; the French doubles with Court in 1973; the Australian doubles with Court in 1973; the Italian doubles with Court in 1968, with Masthoff in 1971 and with Morozova in 1973.

Western grip

A method of gripping the racket.

Wide

A term generally given to a ball that lands out of the playing court beyond the side lines.

Wide-breaking slice

A slice service with so much spin that it pulls the receiver into or beyond the alley.

Wightman Cup

This annual contest between women players of America and England, was inaugurated in 1923. The donor of the trophy (a long slender vase) was Mrs. George Wightman who played in the first series, and has captained the American side several times since. The first contest was held in America, the second in England, and the matches have been staged in alternate countries ever since.

Women

1923	United States	New York
1924	Great Britain	Wimbledon
1925	Great Britain	New York
1926	United States	Wimbledon
1927	United States	New York

1928	Great Britain	Wimbledon
1929	United States	New York
1930	Great Britain	Wimbledon
1931	United States	New York
1932	United States	Wimbledon
1933	United States	New York
1934	United States	Wimbledon
1935	United States	New York
1936	United States	Wimbledon
1937	United States	New York
1938	United States	Wimbledon
1939	United States	New York
1940	Not held	
1941	Not held	
1942	Not held	
1943	Not held	
1944	Not held	
1945	Not held	
1946	United States	Wimbledon
1947	United States	New York
1948	United States	Wimbledon
1949	United States	Philadelphia
1950	United States	Wimbledon
1951	United States	Boston
1952	United States	Wimbledon
1953	United States	Rye
1954	United States	Wimbledon
1955	United States	Rye
1956	United States	Wimbledon
1957	United States	Sewickley
1958	Great Britain	Wimbledon
1959	United States	Sewickley
1960	Great Britain	Wimbledon
1961	United States	Chicago

1962	United States	Wimbledon
1963	United States	Cleveland
1964	United States	Wimbledon
1965	United States	Cleveland
1966	United States	Wimbledon
1967	United States	Cleveland
1968	Great Britain	Wimbledon
1969	United States	Cleveland
1970	United States	Wimbledon
1971	United States	Cleveland
1972	United States	Wimbledon
1973	United States	Boston
1974	Great Britain	Deeside
1975	Great Britain	Cleveland
1976	United States	London
1977	United States	Oakland
1978	Great Britain	London
1979	United States	West Palm Beach
1980	United States	London
1981	United States	Chicago
1982	United States	London
1983	United States	Williamsburg
1984	United States	London
1985	United States	Williamsburg
1986	United States	London
1987	United States	Williamsburg
1988	United States	
1989	United States	

Wilander, Mats

Sweden (born 1964) — He became the youngest ever winner of a Grand Slam title (the record has since been beaten by Boris Becker) when he took the French singles at the age of 17(3/4) in 1982. In 1988 he became the best player in the world by winning three of the four

Grand Slam titles, missing out only at Wimbledon, where he has only twice reached as far as the quarter-finals.

Wilding, Anthony

New Zealand (1883-1915) — He won the Wimbledon doubles with Brookes in 1907 and 1914, and with Malcolm Ritchie in 1908 and 1910. He was Australian singles champion in 1906 and 1909, and took the doubles in 1906 with Rodney Heath. He was in the winning Australasian Davis Cup teams (Australia and New Zealand competed together until 1923) in 1907, 1908, 1909, 1911 and 1914, winning 21 of 30 rubbers.

Wimbledon

The oldest and most important tennis championships are held at the All England Tennis and Croquet Club, Wimbledon, London. The first championships were held in 1877.

Wimbledon Tournament Winners

The most celebrated of the world's major championships, the Wimbledon championships were first played in 1877.

Men's Singles

1877	Spencer Gore	UK
1878	Frank Hadow	UK
1879	Rev. John Hartley	UK
1880	Rev. John Hartley	UK
1881	William Renshaw	UK
1882	William Renshaw	UK
1883	William Renshaw	UK
1884	William Renshaw	UK
1885	William Renshaw	UK
1886	William Renshaw	UK
1887	Herbert Lawford	UK
1888	Ernest Renshaw	UK
1889	William Renshaw	UK

1890	Willoughby Hamilton	UK
1891	Wilfred Beddeley	UK
1892	Wilfred Baddeley	UK
1893	Joshua Pim	UK
1894	Joshua Pim	UK
1895	Wilfred Baddeley	UK
1896	Harold Mahoney	UK
1897	Reginald Doherty	UK
1898	Reginald Doherty	UK
1899	Reginald Doherty	UK
1900	Reginald Doherty	UK
1901	Arthur Gore	UK
1902	Lawrence Doherty	UK
1903	Lawrence Doherty	UK
1904	Lawrence Doherty	UK
1905	Lawrence Doherty	UK
1906	Lawrence Doherty	UK
1907	Norman Brookes	Aus
1908	Arthur Gore	UK
1909	Arthur Gore	UK
1910	Tony Wilding	Nz
1911	Tony Wilding	Nz
1912	Tony Wilding	Nz
1913	Tony Wilding	Nz
1914	Norman Brookes	Aus
1919	Gerald Patterson	Aus
1920	Bill Tilden	USA
1921	Bill Tilden	USA
1922	Gerald Patterson	Aus
1923	William Johnston	USA
1924	Jean Borotra	Fra
1925	Rene Lacoste	Fra
1926	Jean Borotra	Fra
1927	Henri Cochet	Fra

1928	Rene Lacoste	Fra
1929	Henri Cochet	Fra
1930	Bill Tilden	USA
1931	Sidney Wood	USA
1932	Ellsworth Vines	USA
1933	Jack Crawford	Aus
1934	Fred Perry	UK
1935	Fred Perry	UK
1936	Fred Perry	UK
1937	Donald Budge	USA
1938	Donald Budge	USA
1939	Bobby Riggs	USA
1940	Not held	
1941	Not held	
1942	Not held	
1943	Not held	
1944	Not held	
1945	Not held	
1946	Yvon Petra	Fra
1947	Jack Kramer	USA
1948	Bob Falkenburg	USA
1949	Ted Schroeder	USA
1950	Budge Patty	USA
1951	Dick Savitt	USA
1952	Frank Sedgman	Aus
1953	Vic Seixas	USA
1954	Jaroslav Drobny	Cze
1955	Tony Trabert	USA
1956	Lew Hoad	Aus
1957	Lew Hoad	Aus
1958	Ashley Cooper	Aus
1960	Neale Fraser	Aus
1961	Rod Laver	Aus
1962	Rod Laver	Aus

1963	Chuck McKinley	USA
1964	Roy Laver	Aus
1965	Roy Emerson	Aus
1966	Manuel Santana	Spa
1967	John Newcombe	Aus
1968	Rod Laver	Aus
1969	Rod Laver	Aus
1970	John Newcombe	Aus
1971	John Newcombe	Aus
1972	Stan Smith	USA
1973	Jan Kodes	Cz
1974	Jimmy Connors	USA
1975	Arthur Ashe	USA
1976	Bjorn Borg	Swe
1977	Bjorn Borg	Swe
1978	Bjorn Borg	Swe
1979	Bjorn Borg	Swe
1980	Bjorn Borg	Swe
1981	John McEnroe	USA
1982	Jimmy Connors	USA
1983	John McEnroe	USA
1984	John McEnroe	USA
1985	Boris Becker	W. Ger
1986	Boris Becker	W. Ger
1987	Pat Cash	Aus
1988	Stefan Edberg	Swe
1989	Boris Becker	W. Ger
1990	Stefan Edberg	Swe

Women's Singles

1884	Maud Watson	UK
1885	Maud Watson	UK
1886	Blanche Bingley	UK
1887	Lottie Dod	UK

1888	Lottie Dod	UK
1889	Blanche Hillyard	UK
1890	Helene Rice	UK
1891	Lottie Dod	UK
1892	Lottie Dod	UK
1893	Lottie Dod	UK
1894	Blanche Hillyard	UK
1895	Charlotte Cooper	UK
1896	Charlotte Cooper	UK
1897	Blanche Hillyard	UK
1898	Charlotte Cooper	UK
1899	Blanche Hillyard	UK
1900	Blanche Hillyard	UK
1901	Charlotte Sterry	UK
1902	Muriel Robb	UK
1903	Dorothea Douglass	UK
1904	Dorothea Douglass	UK
1905	May Sutton	USA
1906	Dorothea Douglass	UK
1907	May Sutton	USA
1908	Charlotte Sterry	UK
1909	Dora Boothby	UK
1910	Dorothea Lambert Chambers	UK
1911	Dorothea Lambert Chambers	UK
1912	Ethel Larcombe	UK
1913	Dorothea Lambert Chambers	UK
1914	Dorothea Lambert Chambers	UK
1915	Not held	
1916	Not held	
1917	Not held	
1918	Not held	
1919	Suzanne Lenglen	Fra
1920	Suzanne Lenglen	Fra
1921	Suzanne Lenglen	Fra

1922	Suzanne Lenglen	Fra
1923	Suzanne Lenglen	Fra
1924	Suzanne McKane	UK
1925	Suzanne Lenglen	Fra
1926	Kathleen Godfree	UK
1927	Helen Wills	USA
1928	Helen Wills	USA
1929	Helen Wills	USA
1930	Helen Wills Moody	USA
1931	Cilly Aussem	Ger
1932	Helen Wills Moody	USA
1933	Helen Wills Moody	USA
1934	Dorothy Round	UK
1935	Helen Wills Moody	USA
1936	Helen Jacobs	USA
1937	Dorothy Round	UK
1938	Helen Wills Moody	USA
1939	Alice Marble	USA
1940	Not held	
1941	Not held	
1942	Not held	
1943	Not held	
1944	Not held	
1945	Not held	
1946	Pauline Betz	USA
1947	Margaret Osborne	USA
1948	Louise Brough	USA
1949	Louise Brough	USA
1950	Louise Brough	USA
1951	Doris Hart	USA
1952	Maureen Connolly	USA
1953	Maureen Connolly	USA
1954	Maureen Connolly	USA
1955	Louise Brough	USA
1956	Shirley Fry	USA

1957	Althea Gibson	USA
1958	Althea Gibson	USA
1959	Maria Bueno	Bra
1960	Maria Bueno	Bra
1961	Angela Mortimer	UK
1962	Karen Susman	USA
1963	Margaret Smith	Aus
1964	Maria Bueno	UK
1965	Margaret Smith	Aus
1966	Billie Jean King	USA
1967	Billie Jean King	USA
1968	Billie Jean King	USA
1969	Ann Jones	UK
1970	Margaret Smith Court	Aus
1971	Evonne Goolagong	Aus
1972	Billie Jean King	USA
1973	Billie Jean King	USA
1974	Christine Evert	USA
1975	Billie Jean King	USA
1976	Christine Evert	USA
1977	Virginia Wade	UK
1978	Martina Navratilova	Cz
1979	Martina Navratilova	Cz
1980	Evonne Goolagong Cawley	Aus
1981	Christine Evert Lloyd	USA
1982	Martina Navratilova	USA
1983	Martina Navratilova	USA
1984	Martina Navratilova	USA
1985	Martina Navratilova	USA
1986	Martina Navratilova	USA
1987	Martina Navratilova	USA
1988	Steffi Graf	W. Ger
1989	Steffi Graf	W. Ger
1990	Martina Navratilova	USA

Men's Doubles

1879	L.R. Erskine, Herbert Lawford	UK
1880	Ernest Renshaw, William Renshaw	UK
1881	Ernest Renshaw, William Renshaw	UK
1882	Rev. John Hertley, R.T. Richardson	UK
1883	C.W. Grinstead, C.E.Welldon	UK
1884	Ernest Renshaw, William Renshaw	UK
1885	Ernest Renshaw, William Renshaw	UK
1886	Ernest Renshaw, William Renshaw	UK
1887	Patrick Bowes-Lyon, Herbert Wilberforce	UK
1888	Ernest Renshaw, William Renshaw	UK
1889	Ernest Renshaw, William Renshaw	UK
1890	Joshua Pim, Frank Stoker	UK
1891	Herbert Baddeley, Wilfred Baddeley	UK
1892	Harry Barlow, Ernest Lewis	UK
1893	Joshua Pim, Frank Stoker	UK
1894	Herbert Baddeley, Wilfred Baddeley	UK
1895	Herbert Baddeley, Wilfred Baddeley	UK
1896	Herbert Baddeley, Wilfred Baddeley	UK
1897	Lawrence Doherty, Reginald Doherty	UK
1898	Lawrence Doherty, Reginald Doherty	UK
1899	Lawrence Doherty, Reginald Doherty	UK
1900	Lawrence Doherty, Reginald Doherty	UK
1901	Lawrence Doherty, Reginald Doherty	UK
1902	Frank Riseley, Sidney Smith	UK
1903	Lawrence Doherty, Reginald Doherty	UK
1904	Lawrence Doherty, Reginald Doherty	UK
1905	Lawrence Doherty, Reginald Doherty	UK
1906	Frank Riseley, Sidney Smith	UK
1907	Norman Brookes (Aus), Anthony Wilding	Nz
1908	Josiah Ritchie (UK), Anthony Wilding	Nz
1909	Arthur Gore, Roper Barrett	UK
1910	Josiah Ritchie (UK), Anthony Wilding	Nz
1911	Max Decugis, Andre Gobert	Fra

		Wimbledon
1912	Charles Dixon, Roper Barrett	UK
1913	Charles Dixon, Roper Barrett	UK
1914	Norman Brookes (Aus), Anthony Wilding	Nz
1915	Not held	
1916	Not held	
1917	Not held	
1918	Not held	
1919	Pat O'Hara Wood, Ronald Thomas	Aus
1920	Charles Garland, Richard Williams	USA
1921	Randolph Lycett, Max Woosnam	UK
1922	James Anderson (Aus), Randolph Lycett	UK
1923	Leslie Godfree, Randolph Lycett	UK
1924	Frank Hunter, Vincent Richards	USA
1925	Jean Borotra, Rene Lacoste	Fra
1926	Jacques Brugnon, Henri Cochet	Fra
1927	Frank Hunter, William Tilden	USA
1928	Jacques Brugnon, Henri Cochet	Fra
1929	William Allison, John Van Ryn	USA
1930	William Allison, John Van Ryn	USA
1931	George Lott, John Van Ryn	USA
1932	Jean Borotra, Jacques Brugnon	Fra
1933	Jean Borotra, Jacques Brugnon	Fra
1934	George Lott, Lester Stoefen	USA
1935	Jack Crawford, Adrian Quist	Aus
1936	Pat Hughes, Raymond Tuckey	UK
1937	Don Budge, Gene Mako	USA
1938	Don Budge, Gene Mako	USA
1939	Ellwood Cooke, Bobby Riggs	USA
1940	Not held	
1941	Not held	
1942	Not held	
1943	Not held	
1944	Not held	
1945	Not held	

1946	Tom Brown, Jack Kramer	USA
1947	Bob Falkenburg, Jack Kramer	USA
1948	John Bromwich, Frank Sedgman	Aus
1949	Ricardo Gonzales, Frank Parker	USA
1950	John Bromwich, Adrian Quist	Aus
1951	Ken McGregor, Frnak Sedgman	Aus
1952	Ken McGregor, Frank Sedgman	Aus
1953	Lew Hoad, Ken Rosewall	Aus
1954	Rex Hartwig, Mervyn Rose	Aus
1955	Rex Hartwig, Lew Hoad	Aus
1956	Lew Hoad, Ken Rosewall	Aus
1957	Gardnar Mulloy, Budge Patty	USA
1958	Sven Davidson, Ulf Schmidt	Swe
1959	Roy Emerson, Neale Fraser	Aus
1960	Rafael Osuna (MEX), Dennis Ralston	USA
1961	Roy Emerson, Neale Fraser	Aus
1962	Bob Hewitt, Fred Stolle	Aus
1963	Rafael Osuna, Antonio Palafox	Mex
1964	Bob Hewitt, Fred Stolle	Aus
1965	John Newcombe,Tony Roche	Aus
1966	Ken Fletcher, John Newcombe	Aus
1967	Bob Hewitt, Frew McMillan	S.Af
1968	John Newcombe, Tony Roche	Aus
1969	John Newcombe, Tony Roche	Aus
1970	John Newcombe, Tony Roche	Aus
1971	Roy Emerson,Rod Laver	Aus
1972	Bob Hewitt,Frew McMillan	S.Af
1973	Jimmy Connors (US),Ilie Nastase	Rom
1974	John Newcombe, Tony Roche	Aus
1975	Vitas Gerulaitis,Sandy Mayer	USA
1976	Brian Gottfried (US), Raul Ramirez	Mex
1977	Ross Case, Geoff Masters	Aus
1978	Bob Hewitt, Frew McMillan	S.Af
1979	Peter Fleming, John McEnroe	USA

1980	Peter McNamara, Paul McNamee	Aus
1981	Peter Fleming, John McEnroe	USA
1982	Peter McNamara, Paul McNamee	Aus
1983	Peter Fleming, John McEnroe	USA
1984	Peter Fleming, John McEnroe	USA
1985	Heinz Gunthardt (Swi) Bela Taroczi	Hun
1986	Mats Wilander, Joakim Nystram	Swe
1987	Ken Flach, Robert Seguro	USA
1988	Ken Flach, Robert Seguro	USA
1989	John Fitzgerald (AUS),Anders Jarryd	Swe
1990	Rich Leach, Jim Pugh	USA

Women's Doubles

1913	Winfred McNair, Dora Boothby	UK
1914	Agnes Morton (UK), Elizabeth Ryan	USA
1915	Not held	
1916	Not held	
1917	Not held	
1918	Not held	
1919	Suzanne Lenglen (Fra), Elizabeth Ryan	USA
1920	Suzanne Lenglen (Fra), Elizabeth Ryan	USA
1921	Suzanne Lenglen (Fra), Elizabeth Ryan	USA
1922	Suzanne Lenglen (Fra), Elizabeth Ryan	USA
1923	Suzanne Lenglen (Fra), Elizabeth Ryan	USA
1924	Hazel Wightman, Helen Wills	USA
1925	Suzanne Lenglen (Fra), Elizabeth Ryan	USA
1926	Mary Browne, Elizabeth Ryan	USA
1927	Helen Wills, Elizabeth Ryan	USA
1928	Peggy Saunders, Phyllis Watson	UK
1929	Peggy Michell, Phyllis Watson	UK
1930	Helen Moody (nee Wills), Elizabeth Ryan	USA
1931	Dorothy Barron, Phyllis Mudford	UK
1932	Doris Metaxa (Fra), Josane Sigart	Bel
1933	Simone Mathieu (Fra), Josane Sigart	Bel

1934	Simone Mathieu (Fra), Billie Yorke	UK
1935	Freda James, Kay Stammers	UK
1936	Freda James, Kay Stammers	UK
1937	Simone Mathieu (Fra), Billie Yorke	UK
1938	Sarah Fabyan, Alice Marble	USA
1939	Sarah Fabyan, Alice Marble	USA
1940	Not held	
1941	Not held	
1942	Not held	
1943	Not held	
1944	Not held	
1945	Not held	
1946	Louise Brough, Margaret Osborne	USA
1947	Doris Hart, Pat Todd	USA
1948	Louise Brough, Margaret Du Pont	USA
1949	Louise Brough, Margaret Du Pont	USA
1950	Louise Brough, Margaret Du Pont	USA
1951	Shirley Fry, Doris Hart	USA
1952	Shirley Fry, Doris Hart	USA
1953	Shirley Fry, Doris Hart	USA
1954	Louise Brough, Margaret Du Pont	USA
1955	Angela Mortimer, Anne Shilcock	UK
1956	Angela Buxton (UK), Althea Gibson	USA
1957	Althea Gibson, Darlene Hard	USA
1958	Maria Bueno (Bra), Althea Gibson	USA
1959	Jean Arth, Darlene Hard	USA
1960	Maria Bueno (Bra) Darlene Hard	USA
1961	Karen Hantze, Billie Jean Moffitt	USA
1962	Billie Jean Moffit, Karen Susman	USA
1963	Maria Bueno (Bra), Darlene Hard	USA
1964	Margaret Smith, Lesley Turner	Aus
1965	Maria Bueno (Bra), Billie Jean Moffitt	USA
1966	Maria Bueno (Bra), Nancy Richey	USA
1967	Rosemary Casals, Billie Jean King	USA

1968	Rosemary Casals, Billie Jean King	USA
1970	Rosemary Casals, Billie Jean King	USA
1971	Rosemary Casals, Billie Jean King	USA
1972	Billie Jean King (USA), Betty Stove	Hol
1973	Rosemary Casals, Billie Jean King	USA
1974	Evonne Goolagong (Aus), Peggy Michel	USA
1975	Ann Kiyomura (USA), Kazuko Sawamats	Jap
1976	Christine Evert (USA), Martina Navratilova	Cz
1977	Helen Cawley (Aus) , Jonne Russell	USA
1978	Kerr Reid, Wendy Turnbull	Aus
1979	Billie Jean King (USA), Martina Navratilova	Cz
1980	Kathy Jordan, Anne Smith	USA
1981	Martina Navratilova (Cz), Pam Shriver	USA
1982	Martina Navratilova (USA), Pam Shriver	USA
1983	Martina Navratilova (USA), Pam Shriver	USA
1984	Martina Navratilova (USA), Pam Shriver	USA
1985	Kathy Jordan (USA), Liz Smylie	Aus
1986	Martina Navratilova (USA), Pam Shriver	USA
1987	Claudia Kohde-Kilsch (W. Ger), Helena Sukova	Cz
1988	Steffi Graf (W. Ger), Gabriella Sabatini	Arg
1989	Jana Novotna, Helena Sukova	Cz
1990	Jana Novotna, Helena Sukova	Cz

Mixed Doubles

1913	Hope Crip, Agnes Tuckey	UK
1914	James Parke, Ethel Larcombe	UK
1915	Not held	
1916	Not held	
1917	Not held	
1918	Not held	
1919	Radolph Lycett (UK), Elizabeth Ryan	USA
1920	Gerald Paterson (Aus), Suzanne Lenglen	Fra

1921	Randolph Lycett (UK), Elizabeth Ryan	USA
1922	Pat O'Hara Wood (USA), Suzanne Lenglen	Fra
1923	Randolph Lycett (UK), Elizabeth Ryan	USA
1924	Brian Gilbert, Kathleen McKane	UK
1925	Jean Borotra, Suzanne Lenglen	Fra
1926	Leslie Godfree, Kathleen Godfree	UK
1927	Frank Hunter, Elizabeth Ryan	USA
1928	Pat Spence (S.Af), Elizabeth Ryan	USA
1929	Frank Hunter, Helen Wills	USA
1930	Jack Crawford (Aus), Elizabeth Ryan	USA
1931	George Lott, Anna Harper	USA
1932	Enrique Maier (Spa), Elizabeth Ryan	USA
1933	Gottfried von Cramm, Hilda Krahwinkel	Ger
1934	Ryuki Miki (Jap), Dorothy Round	UK
1935	Fred Perry, Dorothy Round	UK
1936	Fred Perry, Dorothy Round	UK
1937	Don Budge, Alice Marble	USA
1938	Don Budge, Alice Marble	USA
1939	Bobby Riggs, alice Marble	USA
1940	Not held	
1941	Not held	
1942	Not held	
1943	Not held	
1944	Not held	
1945	Not held	
1946	Tom Brown, Louise Brough	USA
1947	John Bromwich (Aus), Louise Brough	USA
1948	John Bromwich (Aus), Louise Brough	USA
1949	Eric Sturgess, Sheila Summers	S.Af
1950	Eric Sturgess (S.Af), Louise Brough	USA
1951	Frank Sedgman (Aus), Doris Hart	USA
1952	Frank Sedgman (Aus), Doris Hart	USA
1953	Vic Seixas, Doris Hart	USA
1954	Vic Seixas, Doris Hart	USA

	Wimbledon
1955 Vic Seixas, Doris Hart	USA
1956 Vic Seixas, Shirley Fry	USA
1957 Mervyn Rose (Aus), Darlene Hard	USA
1958 Bob Howe, Lorraine Coghlan	Aus
1959 Rod Laver (Aus), Darlene Hard	USA
1960 Rod Laver (Aus), Darlene Hard	USA
1961 Fred Stolle, Lesley Turner	Aus
1962 Neale Fraser (Aus), Margaret Du Pont	USA
1963 Ken Fletcher, Margaret Smith	Aus
1964 Fred Stolle, Lesley Turner	Aus
1965 Ken Fletcher, Margaret Smith	Aus
1966 Ken Fletcher, Margaret Smith	Aus
1967 Owen Davidson (Aus), Billie Jean King	USA
1968 Ken Fletcher, Margaret Court	Aus
1969 Fred Stolle (Aus), Ann Jones	UK
1970 Ilie Nastase (Rom), Rosemary Casals	USA
1971 Owen Davidson (Aus), Billie Jean King	USA
1972 Ilie Nastase (Rom), Rosemary Casals	USA
1973 Owen Davidson (Aus), Billie Jean King	USA
1974 Owen Davidson (Aus), Billie Jean King	USA
1975 Marty Riessen (USA), Margaret Court	Aus
1976 Tony Roche (Aus), Francoise Durr	Fra
1977 Bob Hewitt, Greer Stevens	S. AF
1978 Frew McMillan (S.Af), Betty Stove	Hol
1979 Bob Hewitt, Greer Stevens	S.AF
1980 John Austin, Tracy Austin	USA
1981 Frew McMillan (S.Af), Betty Stove	Hol
1982 Kevin Curren (S.Af), Anne Smith	USA
1983 John Lloyd (UK), Wendy Turnbull	Aus
1984 John Lloyd (UK), Wendy Turnbull	Aus
1985 Paul McNamee (Aus), Martina Navratilova	USA
1986 Ken Flach, Kathy Jordan	USA
1987 Jeremy Bates, Jo Durie	UK

1988	Sherwood Stewart, Zina Garrison	USA
1989	Jim Pugh (USA), Jana Novotna	Cz
1990	Rick Leach, Zina Garrison	USA

Wimbledon streaks

Between 1927-38, Helen Wills Moody set the longest singles winning streak with 50 matches. Sweden's five-time champion Bjorn Borg holds the men's record for the most consecutive matches won at Wimbledon, with 41.

Women's International Series

As with the men, so women have had an International championship played after a season-long series of tournaments. First held in 1977, it was not held after 1984.

Singles

1977	Chris Evert	USA
1978	Chris Evert	USA
1979	Martina Navratilova	Cz
1980	Tracy Austin	USA
1981	Tracy Austin	USA
1982	Martina Navratilova	USA
1983	Martina Navratilova	USA
1984	Martina Navratilova	USA

Doubles

1977	Francoise Durr (Fra), Wirginia Wade	UK
1978	Billie Jean King (USA), Martina Navratilova	Cz
1979	Billie Jean King (USA), Martina Navratilova	Cz
1980	Rosemary Casals (USA), Wendy Turnbull	Aus
1981	Martina Navratilova (Cz), Pam Shriver	USA
1982	Martina Navratilova, Pam Shriver	USA
1983	Martina Navratilova, Pam Shriver	USA
1984	Martina Navratilova, Pam Shriver	USA

Wood courts

Because the wood would tend to warp and deteriorate if exposed to weather wood courts are limited to indoor use. A wood surface requires some maintenance, is relatively expensive to construct, and generally produces a very fast and low ball bounce; consequently less costly and more appealing surfaces are available for play.

Wood stroke

A stroke in which the ball impacts the frame instead of the strings.

World Championship Tennis

World Championship Tennis incorporated (W.C.T.) was founded in 1967 to promote professional tennis.

Winners

1971	Ken Rosewall	Aus
1972	Ken Rosewall	Aus
1973	Stan Smith	USA
1974	John Newcombe	Aus
1975	Arthur Ashe	USA
1976	Bjorn Borg	Swe
1977	Jimmy Connors	USA
1978	Vilas Gerulaitas	USA
1979	John McEnroe	USA
1980	Jimmy Connors	USA
1981	John McEnroe	USA
1982	Ivan Lendl	Cz
1983	John McEnroe	USA
1984	John McEnroe	USA
1985	Ivan Lendl	Cz
1986	Anders Jarryd	SWE
1987	Miloslav Mecir	Cz
1988	Boris Becker	W. Ger
1989	John McEnroe	USA

Doubles

1973	Bob Lutz, Stan Smith	USA
1974	Bob Hewitt, Frew McMillan	S.Af
1975	Brian Gottfried (USA), Raul Ramirez	Mex
1976	Wojtek Fibak (Pol), Tom Okker	Hol
1977	Vijay Amritraj (India), Dick Stockton	USA
1978	Wojtek Fibak (Pol), Tom Okker	Hol
1979	Peter Fleming, John McEnroe	USA
1980	Brian Gottfried (USA), Raul Ramirez	Mex
1981	Peter McNamara, Paul McNamee	Aus
1982	Heinz Gunthardt (Swe), Balazs Taroczy	Hun
1983	Heinz Gunthardt (Swe), Balazs Tarocz	Hun
1984	Pavel Slozil, Tomas Smid	Cz
1985	Ken Flach, Robert Seguso	USA
1986	Heinz Gunthardt (Swe), Balazs Taroczy	Hun
1987	Stefan Edberg, Anders Jarryd	Swe
1990	Rick Leach, Jim Pugh	USA

World Team Cup

Formerly known as the Nations Cup, it is an eight-nation men's team event. First held in Kingston, Jamaica, in 1975.

Winners

1975	USA
1978	Spain
1979	Australia
1980	Argentina
1981	Czechoslovakia
1982	USA
1983	Spain
1984	USA
1985	USA
1986	France
1987	Czecholsovakia
1988	Sweden

1989 W. Germany
1990 Yugoslavia

Wrist action
The "action" imparted by the wrist to any stroke.

Wrong footing
A shot aimed at the spot from which the opponent made his last stroke with the hope of surprising him and forcing him to turn clumsily.

Y

Youngest champion

Michael Chang eclipsed Boris Becker to become, at 17 years 3(1/2) months, the youngest male Grand Slam champion at the 1989 French Open.

Z

Zip area
The 30 cm (12 in) (approximately) before and after ball and racket make contact, the most important part of the swing of any stroke.